"Imagine being slowly lowered into a cave, against your will. The light fades, and the rock walls close in. You find yourself alone in complete darkness, lost, distressed, agitated, and maybe suicidal. This is the experience of depression. Imagine that a knowledgeable, kind, and thoughtful person appears with survival supplies, and even more important, a flashlight and map to lead you out of this terrifying place. Imagine no more. *Depression: A Guide for the Newly Diagnosed* brings an invaluable map and light for those struggling with depression, the illness most likely to strike any of us during our lives. Buy it. Keep it handy for yourself and those you love."

> —J. Anderson Thomson, Jr., MD, staff psychiatrist at
> the University of Virginia Elson Student Health Center
> and coauthor of *Facing Bipolar*

"This is a straightforward, helpful, and easy-to-read guide for the depressed person."

> —Myrna Weissman, PhD, coauthor of *Interpersonal Psychotherapy for Depressed Adolescents* and *A Clinician's Quick Guide to Interpersonal Psychotherapy*

"Depression is a treatable condition, but a complex one that requires those afflicted to understand what they are facing and what they need to do to get better. In this highly accessible book, Lee Coleman guides the reader through the complexity in a comforting and straightforward way, addressing issues of diagnosis, treatment, and maintaining recovery. If you have depression and are confused about what to do, I highly recommend you start your path to wellness by reading this book."

—Gregg Henriques, PhD, professor of clinical psychology at James Madison University and author of *A New Unified Theory of Psychology*

"The book is sufficiently comprehensive, yet concise and accessible enough for almost any mental health practitioner to recommend to clients who are experiencing depression. It enables any reader who experiences depression to join in their own treatment as an informed and empowered participant. The author integrates insights from the extensive professional literature on depression and treatment effectiveness with wisdom and sensitivity gained in his own clinical practice to provide a useful, straightforward orientation to depression treatment."

—Karen Maitland Schilling, PhD, professor emerita of psychology at Miami University

Depression

A GUIDE *for*
THE NEWLY
DIAGNOSED

Lee H. Coleman, PhD, ABPP

New Harbinger Publications, Inc.

Publisher's Note

Care has been taken to confirm the accuracy of the information presented and to describe generally accepted practices. However, the authors, editors, and publisher are not responsible for errors or omissions or for any consequences from application of the information in this book and make no warranty, express or implied, with respect to the contents of the publication.

The authors, editors, and publisher have exerted every effort to ensure that any drug selection and dosage set forth in this text are in accordance with current recommendations and practice at the time of publication. However, in view of ongoing research, changes in government regulations, and the constant flow of information relating to drug therapy and drug reactions, the reader is urged to check the package insert for each drug and consult with their health care provider for any change in indications and dosage and for added warnings and precautions. This is particularly important when the recommended agent is a new or infrequently employed drug.

Some drugs and medical devices presented in this publication may have Food and Drug Administration (FDA) clearance for limited use in restricted research settings. It is the responsibility of the health care provider to ascertain the FDA status of each drug or device planned for use in their clinical practice.

Distributed in Canada by Raincoast Books

Copyright © 2012 by Lee Coleman
       New Harbinger Publications, Inc.
       5674 Shattuck Avenue
       Oakland, CA 94609
       www.newharbinger.com

Cover design by Amy Shoup; Text design by Michele Waters-Kermes; Acquired by Melissa Kirk; Edited by Will DeRooy

Library of Congress Cataloging-in-Publication Data on file with publisher

Printed in the United States of America

14 13 12

10 9 8 7 6 5 4 3 2 1   First printing

CONTENTS

ACKNOWLEDGMENTS

I want to thank my wonderful friend and colleague Jon Kaplan for telling me about the opportunity to write this book for New Harbinger; it wouldn't have happened without you, man. Melissa Kirk and Nicola Skidmore at New Harbinger, you've been amazing editors, and I'm so grateful for your feedback and patience—not to mention your willingness to take a chance on me. Will DeRooy, thanks so much for your outstanding copyediting.

Mom and Dad, I wish you could have been around to see this hit the shelves. I love you and miss you both dearly. Grant, Katie, Thomas, James, Caroline, Kaye, Adam, Hunter, David, and Kellye—thank you for being my family. I love you so much.

Special thanks to my friends and colleagues at the Caltech Counseling Center for all your support and encouragement while

I was writing. Also, many thanks to the staff of the psychology departments at the University of Alabama and Miami University; the Miami University Student Counseling Center; the University of Virginia CAPS; Boston College UCS; and Ohio University CPS for the best training I could ever have asked for. Karen Maitland Schilling, thanks especially for giving me such a love for interpersonal therapy.

Dan and Karen, I'm especially thankful for your support and understanding when I was sometimes too busy writing to talk. Bridget, thanks for being such an encouraging and supportive friend. Bill Gianesello, Debbie Dunphy, David Loy, Leslie Johnson, and John Garske, thank you for being there for me. Massive thanks also to the wonderful people at Against the Stream for letting me be part of your gloriously funky family.

Most of all, Lani, William, and David, this is for you. I know that all those nights I spent holed up in my office were no fun for you, but somehow you always understood. I love you more than anything else in the entire world.

INTRODUCTION

I'm in the fortunate position of making a living by supervising and training future psychologists. It's a joy and a huge responsibility that I take very seriously, and I often reflect on what lessons I want my supervisees to take with them into their professional lives. There's the usual advice for them to be fully present with their clients, take care of themselves, avoid burnout, and so on. When it comes to their clinical work, though, there's one particular message I've come to see as more important than just about any other: *don't underestimate how serious depression is.*

Depression is hard to cope with, even with excellent treatment. But the sad reality is that the vast majority of people with depression won't get a proper diagnosis or adequate treatment. Even those who get treatment often aren't prepared for the risk of recurrence, leaving them feeling demoralized and hopeless if they get depressed again. It's a worldwide health crisis and a tragedy.

This book is my attempt to turn the tide, one person at a time. If you've recently been diagnosed with depression, or if you think that you may be depressed, I want you to have the very best support and treatment that you can get. I'll talk about making sure that you get a proper diagnosis, including a medical evaluation to rule out other possible problems; finding a mental health professional and deciding what kind of treatment you want to pursue; and managing the day-to-day symptoms that can make life so hard. Most important, I'll also talk about how you can manage the feelings of hopelessness and despair that can plant the seeds of suicidal thoughts.

It's one thing to read about the hellish swamp of depression, and it's quite another to go through it. I've been there too, and if you're depressed I know that you might view a book like this with deep skepticism that things could ever be any better. I'd never ask you to take something on blind faith, which is why I've drawn from the vast body of research on depression to give the single message that there really is hope: in most cases, depression is very treatable. It will take time, effort, and patience on your part, but I want you to have realistic hope and to realize that the journey through depression is always worth it.

CHAPTER 1

WHAT IS
DEPRESSION?

Depression is the most common mental health condition in the United States; up to one in five women and one in ten men will experience it in their lifetimes. Because it's so prevalent, it's sometimes called the common cold of psychiatric illnesses. Depression is much more serious than a cold, though, because it can affect just about every part of your life, from your mood to the way you see the world. The world can look bleak; life stops feeling interesting and enjoyable; and you might even believe that life is no longer worth living. Depression affects different people in different ways, but there are some general patterns that hold true for most people who are dealing with it. Learning the common symptoms can be a good way to begin understanding what depression is and how it can affect your life.

COMMON SYMPTOMS OF DEPRESSION

People with depression usually experience several of the symptoms listed below at the same time. When making a diagnosis, mental health professionals try to determine how many of these symptoms you have and how severe they are. Loosely speaking, having five or more of these symptoms for more than a couple of weeks suggests depression. Keep in mind, though, that any one symptom by itself is not necessarily a cause for concern. It's only when numerous symptoms interfere with your life that you need to be concerned. Also remember that only a trained professional can diagnose depression reliably. I'll talk some more in chapter 2 about how to make sure you're getting an accurate diagnosis.

Sad mood. Not surprisingly, most people who are depressed notice that their mood is sadder than usual. They might have a good day every now and then, but people with depression often struggle with powerful feelings of sadness or even emptiness. Even when they're with loved ones or doing things they used to enjoy, depressed people can feel sad and unable to enjoy what's going on around them.

Loss of interest. It's easy for people with depression to lose interest in the things they used to enjoy. When you're depressed, you might not enjoy talking with your friends as much as you used to, or listening to your favorite music might feel pointless instead of relaxing. Your work, relationships, and activities probably don't seem as enjoyable anymore. You might even not feel interested in sex anymore.

Lower energy. When you're depressed, it can feel hard to do your work, talk with your friends or family, or even get out of bed in the morning. Other people might notice that you seem tired or slowed down. It's not unusual for your sleep to be affected as well; some depressed people begin struggling with insomnia and can't stay asleep, and others might begin sleeping more than usual.

Trouble thinking. Along with reduced energy, it's common for depressed people to experience reduced mental speed. When you're depressed, you may easily become indecisive and feel overwhelmed in the face of even basic decisions, like what to wear for the day or what to eat. Even decisions that used to feel simple may become so paralyzing that you just want to stay in bed all day.

Changes in appetite. Many depressed people lose their appetite because food just doesn't seem as appealing as it used to. A smaller number of people with depression have increased appetite and eat much more than they used to because they find it comforting. Not surprisingly, these appetite changes can lead to a change in weight. In chapter 5 I'll talk about taking good care of yourself even when you don't feel very hungry or if you're relying too much on food to comfort yourself.

Guilt and self-criticism. Depressed people often feel bad about themselves to a degree that's out of proportion to their actual behavior. It's not surprising to feel mad or disappointed in yourself if you're struggling to maintain your normal routine, and some people even blame themselves for being lazy. In more extreme cases of depression, some people blame themselves for things that obviously aren't their fault—even other people's problems. It's as though the depressed person is convinced that he is bad and will easily believe ideas that confirm this view.

Isolation. Depressed people often want to be alone and might become socially isolated. They don't find it fun to be with friends or family anymore, or they might even worry that they'll just bring those people down. It's easy for someone with depression to fall out of contact with friends and stop calling or staying in touch. This is a difficult problem because isolation tends to worsen other depressive symptoms, and it can be hard for a depressed person to find the energy to be around other people.

Thoughts of death or suicide. Most seriously, depressed people think differently about the world—often in ways that are gloomy or bleak. Tragically, it's common for depressed people to have thoughts of death or suicide because they feel so worthless. The feelings of guilt, self-hatred, hopelessness, and worthlessness can make life feel unbearable, and suicide can begin to feel like the only way out. I'll talk in chapter 6 about managing the suicidal risk that can accompany being depressed and how you can monitor your own risk and ask for help before that risk becomes too great. Even though obviously not everyone who is depressed goes on to take their life, the fact is that most suicide victims were dealing with depression or another mental illness.

HOW DO YOU KNOW YOU'RE NOT JUST IN A SAD MOOD?

After learning about the symptoms of their depression, some people think that depression is just another name for being sad and therefore it's no big deal. It's true that everyone gets sad sometimes; it's completely normal and a necessary part of life. Depression is about more than just being in a sad mood, though, in some very important ways. The sad mood that comes with depression is usually more intense and probably feels out of proportion to how things are going in your life. It also lasts longer. Being sad or down for a day or even a few days is normal—we've all been there—but when you've felt that way most of the time for more than a couple of weeks, there's some cause for concern.

WHAT ABOUT GRIEF?

If you've had a loved one die or leave you, grief is a natural reaction, and it can feel very similar to depression. One important difference, though, is that grieving people are sad about the loss of the person who died or left, whereas depressed people feel bad about themselves. Sigmund Freud noted this difference in his classic paper "Mourning and Melancholia" (1917), in which he said that when you're grieving the world feels empty, but when you're depressed *you* feel empty. Grieving over someone we miss is healthy, and the sadness lifts once we learn how to live our lives without that person. Depression, though, doesn't bring a sense of closure and doesn't easily lift by itself.

7

Finally, remember that depression is about more than just your mood. When you're just having a bad day, you're probably still able to work, play, and do other things like you usually do. With depression, though, the effect is serious and widespread. Just as I mentioned in the section on symptoms above, depression can affect your sleep, your appetite, your concentration, your ability to think, and even the way you think. It's never just as simple as being sad.

WHY IS DEPRESSION SO SERIOUS?

Because depression affects so many parts of your life, it's extremely serious by any measure. The World Health Organization estimates that depression is the world's leading cause of disability when measured by the years lived with a disability (Moussavi et al. 2007). It has serious effects on your health, your work, the way you think, and your relationships. Let's explore some of the most common ways that depression can affect your life.

Health Consequences

In terms of health, people with depression tend to have a higher incidence of many major medical problems, including coronary artery disease (Kwahaja et al. 2009) and diabetes (Pan et al. 2010). Worse, people with depression seem to have more complications with various medical conditions, making them harder to treat. The result is that depression can lead to a higher rate of impairment or death due to illness, higher health care spending, and more time lost from work and other activities.

Interpersonal Consequences

Depression seems to be associated with certain types of interpersonal problems, such as being overly dependent on others and constantly seeking reassurance (Joiner 2002). Depression causes marriages and other romantic relationships to suffer, and the nondepressed partner may feel burdened as well. These kinds of interpersonal problems may play a role in bringing about depression in the first place, and of course these problems may also get worse once someone is depressed.

Psychological Consequences

One of the hardest parts of depression is the way it can make you feel weak—not just because you have low energy, but because part of you feels as though you should be able to just "snap out of it." Lots of people think that because we can't see depression on a medical scan or diagnose it with a blood test, it's not real. This is a damaging way of thinking about depression, not only because it's not true, but also because it makes some people think their depression is "all just in their head" and become reluctant to seek treatment. Worst of all, some people become so depressed that they can't imagine that life will improve and, ultimately, they commit suicide.

YOU'RE NOT ALONE, AND THERE'S CAUSE FOR HOPE!

After reading how serious depression can be, you're probably wondering whether there's any good news—and there is. Depression is very treatable for most people. If there's just one message you take away from this book, it should be that depression can and should be treated. This book will focus on things you can do to help yourself from day to day, including being an advocate for yourself in getting a proper diagnosis and proper treatment.

Most people who seek treatment get better, and they get better much more quickly than people who don't seek treatment. On average, someone experiencing depression for the first time can expect to stay depressed for about eight to twelve months without treatment. With treatment, however, most people begin to show significant improvement in about eight weeks (Boland and Keller 2002). Seeking treatment now is also important when it comes to reducing the likelihood of future depressive episodes. The sad fact is that depression tends to recur for most people. I'll talk more about this later, but with proper early treatment, you can reduce the risk of future depression.

You may feel skeptical or even pessimistic that anything can help you. You may have already tried several things that just didn't help, or you might even be feeling generally pessimistic or hopeless. Even if you're feeling pessimistic, consider that it may be the depression itself that's making you pessimistic, and so it may take treating the disorder first in order to change your thinking. That may be frustrating, especially if you like to think things through in a lot of detail before making a decision—but once you're depressed, it can take a long time for feelings of pessimism to subside on their own.

If you've tried treatment for depression before and it didn't work as you had hoped, you should consider whether your depression was treated properly. Fewer than half of depressed people receive proper diagnosis and treatment (González et al. 2010). I'll talk in chapter 2 about making sure that you get an accurate diagnosis, which is vital because it helps you to select the proper treatment.

If you were diagnosed and treated properly but your depression still didn't remit, don't despair! Depression can be tenacious, and what works for one person might not work for another. You've got options, and there are different kinds of treatment you can pursue, which will be discussed in chapter 3.

HOW DID YOU GET THIS WAY?

It's natural to wonder how you got depressed, but before answering that question, you need to know that depression isn't your fault. This question is useful only in helping you understand yourself better—not as a source of blame. Depression isn't due to weakness or laziness, and it's not a reflection of what kind of person you are. You didn't do anything to bring this on yourself—but there *are* things you can do to get better.

Remember that depression is an illness. Because we can't detect depression with a blood test or an X-ray, though, some people minimize their symptoms—or worse, they blame themselves for not being able to "snap out of it." You may have thought, or may have been told, that depression is "all in your head," so you should just be able to be strong and get better. I want to encourage you to fight these beliefs. As I often remind my clients, if it were that simple, you'd have done it already.

You've probably heard the phrase "nature versus nurture" in discussions about how certain illnesses arise. Like most mental illnesses, depression is due to a combination of genetics and environment and involves both biological and psychological factors.

Biological Factors in Depression

There seems to be an inherited component to the disorder, and there are numerous medical conditions that can make these inherited tendencies express themselves. I'll cover some of the basic medical and biological phenomena that play a role in why some people get depressed.

FAMILY HISTORY

Mental health professionals say that depression tends to run in families, but what does this mean? Well, if one (or both) of your parents had depression, you probably have a higher risk of becoming depressed at some point in your life. It's not all due to genetics (and it's not all due to the way you were raised, either): You don't inherit depression, and there's no single gene responsible for depression. Instead, clinicians say that people inherit a vulnerability to depression and that certain life circumstances can trigger a depressive episode among those people who are vulnerable.

Right now, scientists estimate that about 20 to 45 percent of depression's effects are due to genetic components (Wallace, Schneider, and McGuffin 2002).

MEDICAL CAUSES

When you're seeking treatment for possible depression, one of the first things you'll want to do is make sure that your symptoms aren't due to a medical condition. This occurrence is more common than you might suspect, and it's one of the reasons I recommend that you begin the diagnostic process with a visit to your physician or a psychiatrist, either of whom can diagnose medical conditions. Many medical conditions, from thyroid problems to hormonal imbalances, can mimic or worsen the symptoms of depression. This subject is covered in detail in the next chapter.

SUBSTANCE-INDUCED CAUSES

Certain substances can mimic the symptoms of depression or can make a depressive episode worse. As part of getting better, it's especially important that you be honest with your doctor or therapist about any substances you take, including prescription medications, recreational drugs, herbal medications, and alcohol. Alcohol is a central nervous system depressant that can make it harder to recover from a depressive episode. Everyone's tolerance for alcohol varies, but you need to talk with your doctor about how to cut down or even stop drinking while you're trying to recover from a depressive episode. I'll cover this in more detail in chapter 8.

CHEMICAL CAUSES

You've probably heard people say that depression is due to a "chemical imbalance." Even though this can be an oversimplification, depressed people do show certain patterns in their brain chemistry. Chemicals called *neurotransmitters* help brain cells carry information from one to another, and though a thorough discussion of brain chemistry is beyond the scope of this book, depressed people tend to improve when levels of certain neurotransmitters (such as serotonin, norepinephrine, or dopamine) increase.

Psychological Factors in Depression

In addition to these medical factors, there are several psychological attributes that can trigger a depressive episode. These factors usually involve how you think about and feel about significant stressful events in your life. It's not just the things that happen to us—it's how we think about those things. Even factors that would be stressful to anyone will affect different people in different ways depending on how they make sense out of what happened. Let's look at some of these psychological factors in more detail.

REACTION TO A SIGNIFICANT LOSS

What kinds of life events can trigger a depressive episode? Very often, the triggering event is some kind of loss, such as a death, a breakup, a divorce, or even changing jobs. These events are stressful for anyone, but someone vulnerable to depression might have particular trouble coping with these kinds of stress.

Rather than being able to feel resilient and cope well with the loss, depressed people seem to have problems rallying their resources and repairing relationships or seeking out new ones. Sadly, they might even see themselves as having caused or deserved the loss somehow, even when it's not their fault.

WAYS OF THINKING ABOUT YOURSELF AND THE WORLD

It's important to notice some of the ways that depression can go hand-in-hand with certain ways of thinking about the world. For instance, depressed people tend to blame themselves for things that aren't their fault. They tend to see small problems as evidence of larger problems, and worse, they tend to see problems as unlikely to change. Even when you know you might be thinking irrationally, it can be hard to really believe that things could be any other way. It can help to remember that regardless of what caused these negative ways of thinking, your thoughts should improve as you receive treatment.

What should you take away from all of this? Depression is complex and doesn't have a simple cause. It's not enough to say that it's due to nature or nurture, or early childhood experiences, or problems with brain chemistry. What we know is that people seem to inherit a predisposition to become depressed and may be vulnerable to becoming depressed during certain stressful life circumstances.

Despite all of these complex potential causes, I want to argue that it usually doesn't matter very much what initially triggers depression in a person. The treatments I'll discuss are generally effective no matter what the cause. What matters more, I believe, is what *maintains* the depression, because knowing this can help you understand what needs to be different in your life.

TYPES OF DEPRESSION AND OTHER MOOD DISORDERS

Depression doesn't look the same in everyone who has it, and in fact there are different types of depression.

Major Depressive Episode

Let's get some important terminology out on the table. When you're depressed, mental health professionals refer to the time you meet the clinical criteria for the disorder as a *depressive episode*. A depressive episode can last anywhere from a few weeks to several years, but on average it usually lasts about five or six months. The first time you ever have a depressive episode, a mental health professional would diagnose you as having "major depressive disorder, single episode." If you ever get depressed again, your diagnosis would change to "major depressive disorder, recurrent." Once you no longer have the symptoms of depression, you're in *remission*. If you get depressed again soon after entering remission, usually within the first six months, you've had a *relapse*. If you get depressed again after you've been symptom-free for a while, usually more than six months, you've had a *recurrence* of the depression.

Depression with Melancholic Features

Some people with depression will have symptoms that are called *melancholic*. Basically, this means that they find it especially hard to feel any pleasure or take any interest in things that they used to enjoy. Their energy seems particularly low, and they seem to feel worse early in the morning.

Depression with Atypical Features

Even though it's called atypical, this is actually a common subtype of depression. Most people who are depressed experience a certain pattern of symptoms; in part, they typically sleep less and eat less. With *atypical depression*, however, people tend to sleep and eat *more* than they did before becoming depressed. Even though they get more sleep, they still feel fatigued and have low energy. They often report having a heavy feeling in their body, and they seem to be especially sensitive to rejection. Interestingly, unlike with some other types of depression, people with atypical depression seem to be able to temporarily feel happy in response to pleasant external events. Usually, however, it doesn't last long, and the depressive symptoms soon return.

Seasonal Affective Disorder

For some people, their depressive symptoms coincide with the change in seasons in the fall or winter. This is called seasonal affective disorder, or SAD. (*Affect* simply means "mood.") Shorter days, colder weather, and less available daylight all seem to contribute to a depressive episode in some people. Treatment for this unusual variation of depression is interesting; in addition to traditional treatments, it can involve exposure to full-spectrum light for several hours a day to fool the body into thinking it's getting natural sunlight.

Postpartum Depression: The "Baby Blues"

Some women find that the hormonal and emotional changes of pregnancy and childbirth can bring on feelings of depression, leaving them feeling sad, overwhelmed, and worried that they will be unable to care for their baby. Most of the time, these symptoms remit soon after the baby is born, but for some women, the depressive symptoms persist.

Depression with Psychotic Features

A small number of people with depression will also have what are called psychotic features—in other words, they lose touch with reality. People with psychosis can have delusions, highly unusual experiences, or even hallucinations. This type of depression is always very serious, and treatment should always involve consulting with a physician or psychiatrist.

Dysthymic Disorder

One of the other most common mood disorders is called dysthymia, which roughly translates to "sad mood." Think of a major depressive episode with less severe symptoms but that lasts for a longer time, and you'll get a general idea of what dysthymia can feel like. You have to meet the criteria for dysthymia for over two years in order to be properly diagnosed. When someone meets criteria for dysthymia and a major depressive episode at the same time, this is sometimes called "double depression," and it is harder to treat than either disorder alone.

A Word about Bipolar Disorder

You've probably heard of bipolar disorder, formerly called manic depression. For people with this disorder, depression is only half of the story. When a depressive episode is over, they may return to their normal baseline mood, or they might enter a period in which their symptoms paint a picture the exact opposite of depression. Like depression, bipolar disorder affects your mood, your energy, your sleep, and the way you view the world. Unlike depression, however, bipolar disorder is likely to cause you to have a giddy, excited, or irritable mood; be overly energetic and impulsive; need little sleep; and engage in risky behavior without regard for the consequences. People with bipolar disorder might have fleeting but intense interest in many things or even wild, grandiose beliefs, such as that they have magical powers.

This "up" period is called a manic episode (at the more severe end of the spectrum) or a hypomanic episode (at the less severe end of the spectrum). Either one is still a very serious diagnosis. People dealing with a hypomanic episode are often energetic, witty, fun to be around, spontaneous, and joyful. At its worst, though, hypomania or mania can lead to racing thoughts, pressure to keep talking, impulsive actions, a need to engage in risky behavior, and even grandiose thoughts. Sadly, it's common to hear of people in the throes of a manic episode impulsively maxing out their credit cards, engaging in risky sex, believing they have special knowledge or powers, and even becoming delusional or psychotic. Bipolar disorder is extremely serious and can lead to major life problems, arrest, hospitalization, and even suicide.

It's very common for hypomanic or manic episodes to alternate with depressive episodes, sometimes as often as several times a year. If you're depressed, then, it's very important that you find out whether your depressive episode is just one part of a larger pattern of mood changes. An evaluation from a mental health professional will help you assess this possibility and get appropriate treatment. The recommended treatment for bipolar disorder almost always involves taking medication and making important lifestyle changes to minimize the risk of triggering another manic or hypomanic episode.

A full discussion of bipolar disorder is beyond the scope of this book. If you suspect that you have symptoms of bipolar disorder, much of the advice in this book is not appropriate for you, even though you may feel depressed part of the time. Treatment should always involve talking with your physician or psychiatrist about how to manage your symptoms. A practical introduction geared toward young adults (but still appropriate for anyone) is Russ Federman and J. Anderson Thomson Jr.'s excellent recent book, *Facing Bipolar: The Young Adult's Guide to Dealing with Bipolar Disorder.*

SUMMARY

Depression is an extremely common mental health condition that affects not only your mood, but also your body, your thoughts, and the way you experience the world. It doesn't have one simple cause, but people seem to inherit a vulnerability to depression that leads to problems coping with certain difficult life circumstances. It's not your fault—or anyone else's—and the good news is that depression is highly treatable. Sadly, most people with depression don't get a proper diagnosis or adequate treatment. In chapter 2, I'll focus on making sure that you get an accurate diagnosis.

CHAPTER 2

GETTING A CORRECT DIAGNOSIS

If you're wondering whether you might be depressed, it's important that you seek out a correct diagnosis. Over half of people with depression don't receive proper diagnosis and treatment, so I'm going to talk about how you can ensure the best care for yourself.

PROPER DIAGNOSIS MAKES ALL THE DIFFERENCE

Given that this book is aimed at people newly diagnosed with depression, you may have already taken some steps to find out what's going on. If so, that's great; this chapter will offer some suggestions on making sure you're being thorough. If you haven't taken any kind of step toward diagnosis yet, that's fine too; I'll talk about some good first steps you can take.

STEP ONE: GET A MEDICAL CHECKUP

Getting a medical checkup is an excellent place to start. Because many physical ailments can affect your energy level, sleep, appetite, and sex drive, it's important for you to make sure that any problem you're having in these areas isn't due to an undiagnosed illness or medical condition rather than depression. There are actually a number of illnesses that can mimic or even worsen the symptoms of depression. In my experience working with depressed clients, I've seen several people who, after visiting their doctors, turned out to have had an undiagnosed medical condition like hypothyroidism, diabetes, or even a sleep disorder. Getting a clear medical diagnosis first can help identify any medical issues that you should treat—and, in fact, ruling out any medical condition as a cause of depressive symptoms is a necessary step in accurately diagnosing depression.

You should also know that the question of diagnosis is not black and white—you might have depression along with a medical condition, for instance. There are many medical or psychological problems with which depression very commonly co-occurs. The good news is that regardless of any other health or emotional problems you're dealing with at the same time, treating the depression can have beneficial effects. For instance, treating depression can lower the level of the stress hormone cortisol in your blood, and it can also lower your risk of coronary artery disease and other heart problems.

You might also find that your symptoms may suggest that in addition to depression you have another psychiatric diagnosis. This is actually quite common—depression very commonly co-occurs with anxiety disorders, substance abuse, and personality disorders. These are then called *comorbid conditions*, and I'll talk in chapter 8 about managing them effectively. Some people also have comorbid medical disorders such as epilepsy or other neurological problems, and though they're beyond the scope of this book, it will be important for you to discuss these disorders thoroughly with your physician.

Information to Take to Your Physician

In preparing for your visit with your physician or psychiatrist, it will be helpful to fill out this questionnaire and bring it with you. If you have had any of these symptoms for more than two weeks, indicate how often they have been bothering you. This will give your doctor a good understanding of your concerns and will help her to make a more accurate diagnosis. This questionnaire is a public domain instrument called the Patient Health Questionnaire – 9 (PHQ-9), developed by Spitzer, Williams, and Kroenke (2001), and it is widely used to diagnose possible depression.

Indicate how often you have been bothered by each of the following problems over the last two weeks.

1. Little interest or pleasure in doing things:

    Not at all   Several days   More than   Nearly
                                      half the days   every day

2. Feeling down, depressed, or hopeless:

    Not at all   Several days   More than   Nearly
                                      half the days   every day

3. Trouble falling or staying asleep, or sleeping too much:

    Not at all   Several days   More than   Nearly
                                      half the days   every day

4. Feeling tired or having little energy:

    Not at all   Several days   More than   Nearly
                                      half the days   every day

5. Poor appetite or overeating:

    Not at all   Several days   More than   Nearly
                                      half the days   every day

6. Feeling bad about yourself—or that you are a failure or have
    let yourself or your family down:

    Not at all   Several days   More than   Nearly
                                      half the days   every day

7. Trouble concentrating, such as on reading the newspaper or watching TV:

    Not at all   Several days   More than   Nearly
                                          half the days   every day

8. Moving or speaking so slowly that other people could have noticed. Or the opposite—being so fidgety or restless that you have been moving around a lot more than usual:

    Not at all   Several days   More than   Nearly
                                          half the days   every day

9. Thoughts that you would be better off dead or thoughts of hurting yourself in some way:

    Not at all   Several days   More than   Nearly
                                          half the days   every day

10. Finally, if you are experiencing any of the problems above, how difficult have these problems made it for you to do your work, take care of things at home, or get along with other people?

    Not difficult   Somewhat   Very difficult   Extremely
    at all   difficult   difficult

Your physician will review the number and pattern of the symptoms you checked and will use this information in making a diagnosis.

Other Important Information for Your Physician

Next, you should provide the following information on a separate sheet of paper and take it with you to your physician.

CURRENT MEDICATIONS AND DOSAGES

In addition to talking about your symptoms, you'll also want to tell your physician about any medication you're taking, whether it's over-the-counter, prescription, or herbal. Many medications can have unintended effects on your mood, so it will be important to make sure that your depressive symptoms aren't due to such side effects (Rogers and Pies 2008).

ANY OTHER SYMPTOMS OR CONCERNS

Depression often doesn't occur in isolation. I'll talk about this at length in chapter 8, but for now just know that it's very common for depression to occur alongside other psychiatric conditions such as anxiety or alongside medical conditions such as anemia. You can help your doctor make a good diagnosis by listing any other symptoms or problems you've been experiencing. If you're not sure where to begin, just think about the ways in which you haven't felt like yourself lately. You can also ask people you trust whether they've noticed anything different about you.

FAMILY MEDICAL HISTORY

One other important piece of information you can provide your physician is your family history of any psychiatric conditions.

As I mentioned in chapter 1, mood disorders like depression tend to run in families, so your family history can provide critical information. If your grandparents, parents, or any siblings have been depressed before, you might be at slightly higher risk of becoming depressed yourself.

ALCOHOL AND SUBSTANCE USE

In addition to any medication you're taking, it's very important that you tell your physician how much alcohol you typically drink and how often you drink. Likewise, if you use any other drugs or substances, you should be open with your physician. Why? Substance abuse is one of the problems most commonly co-occurring with depression, and it can significantly interfere with your ability to recover from the depression. Many people balk at being open about any illicit substance use because they're worried they'll get in trouble, but your physician isn't going to report you to anyone. Rather, information about your substance use can be critical in making an accurate diagnosis of depression or any other emotional problem—so being honest is in your best interest.

I'm not being judgmental, and this isn't about morals or ethics; it's about committing to get better. If you're using alcohol or certain drugs to excess, this can and will interfere with getting a proper diagnosis. Even worse, in some cases, alcohol or drug use can significantly undermine your efforts to get better. So it's very important for you to be honest with yourself and your physician or therapist about any alcohol or drugs that you use.

By itself, drinking alcohol doesn't have to be a problem; what matters is the effect that your drinking has on your life. When you're dealing with depression, it's easy for even moderate alcohol use to become problematic. This is because alcohol is a central nervous system depressant. That means that alcohol affects your brain to produce feelings of tiredness, a slower heart rate, slowed breathing, muscle relaxation, slowed thinking and reaction time, and similar effects. In small doses these feelings can be pleasant, but if you're depressed, you've probably experienced the "fog" of feeling slowed down, feeling tired, and not thinking clearly. Alcohol can worsen these symptoms and make it even harder to participate in activities in which you feel active and engaged. It's a bad combination, and it's even potentially dangerous. For this reason, I'd encourage you to cut down—or, better yet, cut out alcohol completely—while you're recovering. This doesn't mean cutting it out forever—just for now, while you're recovering from depression.

Additionally, if you're taking antidepressant medication, you should talk carefully with your physician or psychiatrist about your alcohol use. Many antidepressant medications can *potentiate* (that is, strengthen) the effects of alcohol so that your body will react more strongly. On certain medications, even one drink can affect your body like two or more, making it easy to lose track of how your alcohol use is affecting your mood, health, judgment, and thinking. And if you're taking certain medications, such as MAO (monoamine oxidase) inhibitors, certain types of alcohol can cause a potentially fatal drug interaction. You should always check with your physician or psychiatrist about how any medication you're taking can interact with alcohol.

In terms of other substances, marijuana use is common, and some people who are depressed use marijuana to take their mind off their negative feelings. Does marijuana use worsen depression? The research isn't clear. Some studies suggest that marijuana use does not directly worsen your mood, but it can increase feelings of apathy and reduce motivation (Moore et al. 2007; Musty and Kaback 1995). There's little evidence to suggest that marijuana use *improves* depressive symptoms, so in light of the lack of evidence and the risk of becoming more apathetic, I'd advise reducing or stopping marijuana use while you're trying to get better. If you're uncomfortable telling your physician or therapist about your drug use, don't worry—they're not going to report you, and they can help you figure out which symptoms might be due to depression and which might be due to substance use. There are obviously other substances that can affect your mood and functioning while you're depressed; I'll cover this topic more deeply in chapter 8.

WHAT TO EXPECT FROM A VISIT WITH A PHYSICIAN

Because of the way our health care system works, most people are probably more comfortable visiting their family physician first. This can be a great place to start because, as I mentioned earlier, she can begin helping by evaluating you for medical problems, and she can even diagnose your depression. Plus, if you already are acquainted with your physician, you might be more comfortable talking with her than to someone new like a psychologist or psychiatrist.

Even if you start your recovery by visiting your physician, I want to suggest that your journey does not have to end there. Many physicians are skilled at diagnosing depression, but because physicians are often generalists, they may not specialize in recognizing or treating emotional disorders like depression (Mitchell, Vaze, and Rao 2009). It's important, then, that you feel comfortable asking your physician about her experience with treating depression. If your physician doesn't mention talk therapy as a treatment, it's okay to ask for more information about it so that you can make a more fully informed decision.

What kinds of things will your physician want to assess? Depending on your symptoms, she might want to rule out certain medical conditions. Some thyroid problems can create hormonal imbalances that can mimic the symptoms of depression, so be sure to let your physician know if you have any family history of thyroid or other endocrine problems.

Your physician might also ask whether you're getting proper nutrition; in some cases, poor nutrition can negatively affect your mood and energy levels. If you're not sure that you're eating well, your physician can assess your prealbumin level. Prealbumin is a substance that carries hormones and vitamins throughout your body, and low levels suggest a lack of protein and other nutrients. Imbalances in electrolytes like sodium and potassium, which help the body conduct electrical nerve impulses properly, can also affect your neurological functioning. Additionally, anemia, a condition in which red blood cells have trouble transporting oxygen properly, can have a pronounced effect on your mood and energy. Some simple blood tests can help check for these and other conditions.

Because physicians can prescribe medication, they will likely discuss the option of taking antidepressant medication. I'll talk more in the next chapter about what to consider when deciding whether medication is right for you, but for now, some important questions you can ask your physician are:

- What does this medication do?

- How often should I take it?

- How long does it take this medication to begin working, and what kinds of changes should I expect?

- What are the common side effects?

- Are there any effects that should concern me enough to call your office?

- How soon should we meet again to talk about how the medication is working?

- How long will I likely need to stay on this medication?

- After the medical checkup, what are the next steps?

Don't worry about asking questions—it's better to ask them now than to risk uncertainty later. Any competent physician should welcome your questions without getting defensive.

For many people with depression, their treatment begins and ends in their family physician's office. This isn't necessarily bad, but it can be unnecessarily limiting when there are many excellent treatment options available. In addition to seeing your family physician, you might want to consider meeting with a mental health professional who specializes in treating emotional problems like depression.

WHAT TO EXPECT FROM A VISIT WITH A MENTAL HEALTH PROFESSIONAL

Let's talk about the decision to visit a mental health professional— that is, someone other than your primary care physician who specializes in diagnosing and treating emotional and behavioral problems. Perhaps your physician recommended this route, or perhaps you began your search for a diagnosis by meeting with a counselor or therapist. Let's start by distinguishing between two main groups of mental health professionals—those who primarily do talk therapy, and those who primarily prescribe medication.

Psychologists and Other Talk Therapists

There are many kinds of mental health professionals who are qualified to diagnose and treat depression. Some of the most common are (by professional title):

- Clinical psychologists, who usually hold a doctorate in psychology (a PhD or PsyD)

- Licensed clinical social workers (LCSWs)

- Marriage and family therapists (MFTs)

- Licensed professional counselors (LPCs) and mental health counselors (MHCs)

- Psychoanalysts, who usually hold an MD or PhD and usually specialize in providing long-term, in-depth talk therapy

For most of these titles, the professionals must demonstrate to a state licensing board that they have the proper training and education, and they must also pass a state exam for licensure. You should feel comfortable asking a potential therapist about her education, training, and experience diagnosing and treating depression. A competent therapist should welcome your questions without getting defensive.

Depending on where you're seeking services, your therapist might be in training and have a title like "psychology intern." Therapists in training will disclose this fact to you at the beginning of your meeting with them. These therapists are directly supervised by licensed professionals and can provide excellent services under their supervisor's guidance.

For convenience, I'll use the term "therapist" here to refer to any qualified individual providing talk therapy. However, you should know that the designations "therapist," "counselor," and "psychotherapist" by themselves are usually not regulated by state agencies, so this means that anyone can use these descriptions, no matter what their training. If someone uses one of these terms to describe her services without disclosing her degree or professional title, it's okay to ask her for further information about her background and training.

There are some other titles for mental health professionals, depending on which state you live in. I won't try to list all possible titles and qualifications here; just know that you should always feel free to ask any potential therapist about her education, training, and experience.

What to Expect from Meeting with a Therapist

What should you expect from a first visit with a therapist? Your first meeting will probably last from forty-five to ninety minutes, depending on how the therapist practices. Your therapist will want to understand what led you to seek treatment, how long your symptoms have been a problem, what your goals are for therapy, and other aspects of your situation. Your therapist will also want to know more about you than just your problems and thus will probably ask some questions about your family, your work, your relationships, and your health.

By the end of the first meeting, ideally, you should have some ideas about the nature of the problems you're dealing with. Life's problems usually don't lend themselves to simple explanations, but you and your therapist should have some tentative thoughts. Depending on the nature of your concerns, at the end of the first meeting the therapist may or may not be ready to recommend a certain course of treatment. Therapy almost always begins with setting aside a few meetings to understand and identify the core issues. Don't plan on leaving the first meeting with everything being magically fixed; instead, you should expect that you and your therapist should have begun generating some ideas together about how to proceed.

So what is talk therapy all about? I'll go into much more detail in chapter 3, but for now here are some of the main things you should know. Regardless of how your therapist practices, the most important thing is that you feel a connection to her, making you feel that you can be open and honest with her. Having a solid, trusting therapeutic relationship is one of the best assurances that the therapy will go well. If you've met with a therapist a few times and still don't feel that the connection is as good as you'd like it to be, it's okay to bring this up and, if necessary, keep shopping around. You don't have to settle for the first therapist you meet if the connection isn't good.

If you do interview more than one therapist, how can you make a good decision about whom to choose? There's no such thing as a 100-percent perfect fit, but some factors are very important when you're forming your commitment to therapy. For instance, do you generally like your therapist, and do you feel that you can begin to trust her? Does she talk openly and without complicated jargon? How well does she seem to understand you? Invest some time in answering these questions, and respect your thoughts and feelings; if something doesn't feel right, it's okay to keep looking for someone you can work with in a trusting way.

Once a good relationship is in place, what then? There shouldn't be anything mystifying about what your therapist says to you. Your therapist should be able to offer some thoughts on what's maintaining your depression, even if it's not clear what initially triggered it. Once the two of you agree on the nature of the problem, you can go ahead and begin making a plan for what to do about it. Some therapists will call your attention to your style of thinking—for instance, you might believe that saying or doing something poorly means that you're a horrible person—and offer alternative ways of thinking about yourself. Other therapists might frame the problem in terms of problems in your relationships—for instance, you might find it hard to comfortably assert what you need from a romantic partner. What matters is that you and your therapist basically agree on what is maintaining your depression and make a plan for how to change it.

TV and movies would have us believe that therapy consists of someone lying on a couch and free-associating while a silent (usually bearded) older man sits to the side, dutifully scribbling notes on a clipboard. Fortunately, in real life therapy is almost never like this—it should be an engaging conversation that slowly helps you understand more about yourself and what you might begin to do differently. I say slowly because, unlike in movies, therapy isn't about having dramatic "aha!" moments that magically fix everything. Lots of people believe that therapy will focus exclusively on their childhood experiences and will help them realize what early life events triggered their depression. But I want to challenge this stereotype for a few reasons—first, to help you have accurate expectations, but also to suggest that whatever triggered your depression is probably much less important than whatever is maintaining it in your life right now. Besides, something as complex as depression usually can't be attributed to only one or two events in your life. Sure, it's satisfying if you can gain some insight into how you got depressed, but if you don't, that's okay. Don't worry that something's missing from your therapy if you're not sure how you got depressed. It's often more important to focus on your life as it is right now.

Psychiatrists

A psychiatrist is a mental health professional who is a medical doctor. This means that she has a medical degree (MD or DO) and special training in diagnosing and treating emotional disorders or mental illnesses. Some psychiatrists specialize in prescribing medication; some specialize in providing talk therapy; and some do both. If you're meeting with a psychiatrist, then, it's important to ask what services she does and doesn't provide.

What are some good questions to ask a psychiatrist you're considering? First, you should ask whether she provides psychotherapy (that is, talk therapy) in addition to prescribing medication. If she does, you should talk with her clearly about what she offers and what you're looking for. If you're looking primarily for talk therapy, I'd encourage you to ask the same kinds of questions discussed above in the section on psychologists and other talk therapists. If you're looking primarily for medication, I'd encourage you to ask the same kinds of questions discussed above in the section on physicians.

You should also ask yourself whether you prefer meeting with the same person for therapy and medication; some people do prefer that, but others prefer to see separate professionals. Either is fine, but if you're seeing separate professionals, it's important that you sign a release of information form allowing them to communicate with one another about your care.

Many psychiatrists prescribe medication for depression if they believe it's warranted. If you decide to take medication, should your general practitioner or your psychiatrist be the one to prescribe it? I want to suggest that psychiatrists have the edge here because they specialize in the kinds of drugs commonly prescribed for depression and because they have more of a specialty in treating depression. It's not that family physicians aren't competent to prescribe antidepressants or treat depression, but psychiatrists bring to the table an expertise in depression that most general physicians don't have. Also, depression is just a small part of what family physicians see day to day (Mitchell, Vaze, and Rao 2009), whereas psychiatrists see many more people who are depressed and can usually bring more experience to your care.

LOCATING A MENTAL HEALTH PROFESSIONAL

If you have health insurance, I suggest calling your insurance company and asking for some local mental health professionals who are covered under your plan. Most insurance companies maintain a web page that will help you locate local health care providers. Be aware that mental health professionals are sometimes listed in a separate category from primary care physicians. This category is sometimes labeled "behavioral health providers" or "mental health providers." If you live in a densely populated area, searches like these will often return dozens of names, and it can be hard to know where to start. I recommend cross-referencing the list from your insurance company with a list of local providers from a reputable professional organization. If you have a friend or family member who's seen a mental health professional, you might also ask that person for recommendations.

In chapter 10 I'll also direct you to some online resources and provide contact information for numerous professional organizations that can help you find an appropriate therapist.

SUMMARY

Getting the proper treatment for depression starts with getting a proper diagnosis. I recommend that you always begin with a medical examination to rule out possible health problems causing or worsening your symptoms. It's fine if you get this examination through your primary care physician or by meeting with a psychiatrist. If you are still diagnosed with depression even after you've obtained a medical examination, it's extremely important for you to treat this illness. Untreated depression usually lasts longer and is more severe than depression that's treated properly. How can you decide which treatment approach is right for you? I'll talk about treatment options in more detail in chapter 3.

CHAPTER 3

TREATMENTS FOR DEPRESSION

So, once you've made the decision to seek help, what actually happens? How is depression actually treated? In this chapter, I'll cover the most common ways that professionals treat depression so that you can think about what's right for you. Knowing the most common treatments will also help you form realistic expectations about what treatment can and can't do.

PSYCHOTHERAPY

If you've never been in therapy before, your concept of what it's like is probably based on stereotypes you've seen in media.

Cartoons from the *New Yorker* usually depict a bearded older man with glasses who sits silently while a patient lies on a couch, complaining about how bad life is. Movies and TV paint dramatic pictures of therapy in which patients search for the hidden secrets from their childhood that will unlock the keys to their current suffering. Even worse, many movies paint therapists as predators who manipulate and even seduce their patients! Fortunately, none of these represent what therapy is really like. Let's take some time to set the record straight on what therapy is, what it isn't, and what you can expect if you talk with a therapist.

Think of therapy as a very personal conversation—one whose primary focus is helping you understand yourself better. You'll be talking about yourself with someone who has expertise in problems in living and who can, ideally, help you think about yourself in a different way. Because it's a conversation, it takes time for the therapist to understand what your problems and concerns are, and your therapist will usually set aside one to three meetings just so the two of you can make a plan about how to proceed. During this planning stage, most therapists will ask you questions about what brings you in, what kinds of problems you've noticed, and how you think therapy might be able to help you. They'll want to know when your depression started, what you think is maintaining it, whether there's any family history of depression, and other information.

Most therapists don't give direct advice—at least not at first. It's not that they have all the answers and are trying to hold out on you, or are making you jump through hoops to figure everything out yourself; life is complex, and there's not a one-size-fits-all approach to treating depression. Getting advice right away might feel gratifying at first, but any advice given quickly would probably overlook what's unique to your life situation. I mention this so that you won't expect your therapist to sit you down and hand you a road map of everything you need to do to get better. Life is more complex than that, and treating depression is no exception.

So, what can you expect? There are different kinds of psychotherapy for depression, and I want to discuss some of the most common ones so that you can understand where your therapist is probably coming from. It's always okay to ask your therapist how he understands depression and how he typically treats it.

Cognitive Therapy and Cognitive Behavioral Therapy

One of the most common approaches to treating depression focuses on the way that you think. Because it's so focused on your thoughts, it's called cognitive therapy, abbreviated CT. A similar approach that incorporates some additional techniques is called cognitive behavioral therapy, abbreviated CBT. Remember, depression doesn't just affect your mood; it affects how you look at the world, how you look at yourself, and your relationships. Learning about some of the assumptions you make in your thinking can be enormously helpful in your adopting a more effective and realistic view of things. Research has shown that both cognitive therapy and cognitive behavioral therapy are very effective in treating depression (Rupke, Blecke, and Renfrow 2006).

Depressed people tend to look at the world in a particular way. When we're depressed, we tend to believe that when things don't turn out, it's our fault (that is, we think it's because of something internal—within us—instead of due to chance or external situations). We also tend to believe that problems are long-lasting instead of temporary and that they're proof of a larger pattern of problems instead of being situational. For instance, someone who's depressed and forgets a dinner date with a friend would be more likely to think things like "I'm such a forgetful person...I'm always doing things like this, and I probably always will." A cognitive therapist would help this person notice his *automatic negative thoughts* in this situation and explore whether they're really true. Does forgetting one dinner date automatically make someone a forgetful person, and is it useful for him to label himself with names like "forgetful person"? Is it really the case that he always does things like this, or are there many examples from his life that show that most of the time he actually doesn't forget dinner dates? Does it make sense to predict the future and assume he'll always do this sort of thing? If this sounds like talking back to yourself, you're right—it is! I sometimes joke with my clients that this approach is, in a nutshell, "Don't believe everything you think" and that it's worth it to talk back to ourselves.

Cognitive therapists teach depressed people to notice common mistakes in their thinking. These mistakes are sometimes called *cognitive distortions* or *cognitive errors*. We all make them from time to time; it's just that when we're depressed, it's easier to commit some of these errors without realizing it. One common cognitive error, for instance, is called black-and-white thinking; we assume that either things are great or they're a disaster, without ever considering the middle ground. Another one is assuming that when positive things happen it's just luck, while negative things that happen are our fault. It can be interesting to step back and see how our minds play these tricks on us, and I sometimes encourage my clients to make it a game to catch themselves committing some of these cognitive errors.

It's not enough just to notice the errors, though. When I mentioned talking back to ourselves, I meant that we have to replace irrational or ineffective thoughts with more rational, useful ones. Your therapist can be extremely helpful here by suggesting healthier ways of thinking about things. For instance, the person who forgot the dinner date might remind himself that even though this was an undesirable situation, it's not proof that he's inherently a horrible or forgetful person. Reframing the situation like this might sound easy, but it often takes extensive practice to get good at it. With practice, though, it's much easier to undo some of the maladaptive thinking that depression can bring on us.

Interpersonal Psychotherapy (IPT) for Depression

Another approach to treating depression focuses not on our thoughts, but on our relationships. It's called interpersonal psychotherapy for depression, sometimes abbreviated IPT, and it has outstanding research support. I very commonly do IPT with my depressed clients, and most of them find it very practical and effective. What's interesting about IPT is that it doesn't make any claims about what causes depression; in this kind of therapy, it doesn't matter! What does matter is identifying the kinds of life circumstances that maintain the depression from day to day and how they can be changed for the better.

In IPT, your therapist will talk with you about what kinds of life events are going on for you, and you'll explore how they may relate to your depression. IPT recognizes four broad categories of life problems that you might focus on in therapy: role disputes (that is, when you and someone else have different expectations about the relationship); role transitions (that is, getting used to a major life change, such as getting married or losing your job); grief after a death; and general problems relating to other people. By helping you identify and cope with the social triggers of your depression, this type of therapy can help you begin to feel less isolated, more effective, more in control, and more satisfied with your life.

I like doing IPT; it's practical, it doesn't rely on any mysterious concepts, and clients tend to understand it quickly. It enjoys outstanding research support and is considered an empirically supported treatment for depression (Weissman, Markowitz, and Klerman 2007; Mufson et al. 2004; Weissman, Markowitz, and Klerman 2000).

Psychodynamic Therapy

Many therapists practice some variation of what's called psychodynamic therapy. "Psychodynamic" sounds complicated, but it just means that different parts of our lives can be in conflict with each other, causing us problems in life. For instance, how many times have you had to do a report or some other necessary piece of work, but you put it off because you just couldn't bring yourself to do it? That's a conflict between the part of you that wants to work and the part that doesn't. Or perhaps you've met someone you really like, but for reasons you don't fully understand, you can't bring yourself to call him for a second date. Psychodynamic therapy focuses on helping us make sense out of these emotional conflicts so that we can understand ourselves better and have more freedom to choose how we want to respond to life's problems.

With my depressed clients, one of the most common conflicts I see is between the part of them that wants to draw closer to others and the part that wants to pull away. When we open this up to explore it, sometimes the depressed person is convinced that an interaction will just end in rejection, so it's safer not to try in the first place. Not trying gives the person a temporary feeling of safety, and it certainly keeps him from getting hurt if things don't go well, but it comes at the cost of feeling lonely and isolated. Worse, the depressed person misses out on the chance to find out whether things would have gone well. Much of the time, conflicts like this unfold without our even realizing it; often the person with depression isn't even conscious of the fear of being rejected and how he's protecting himself from it. By becoming more aware of these fears, he can think about different ways that he might reasonably protect himself while still being open to taking reasonable risks.

With depression, it's common to find that, without even realizing it, you've been acting as though you're convinced you're a bad person. You might approach other people as though they're not going to like you in the first place, or you might stay in bed a lot because it doesn't feel like anything could go well for you.

Psychodynamic therapy can help you become more aware of assumptions like these and safely question them in a supportive, safe environment. Psychodynamic therapy enjoys a very good research base showing its efficacy with numerous disorders, including depression (Shedler 2010).

Mindfulness and Other Approaches

One of the most promising new developments in psychotherapy is the use of mindfulness-based approaches to treating depression. Mindfulness is not necessarily a separate approach to therapy but rather a way of thinking about your depression. Mindfulness borrows heavily from some Buddhist concepts, but it's not a religious or spiritually focused approach. Rather, it's a way of accepting your depression without trying to overtly change it. This may sound completely backward, but as you'll see in a moment, this approach can lead to significant improvements. Initial research on certain forms of mindfulness-based therapy for depression appears promising not only in reducing symptoms, but also in preventing relapse (Ma and Teasdale 2004; Teasdale et al. 2000).

Depression is painful, and I'm not naively saying that mindfulness can make that pain disappear. Rather, mindfulness helps us become more aware and more accepting of reality as it's unfolding right now, instead of how we wish it could be.

MINDFUL AWARENESS

Mindfulness just means nonjudgmentally paying attention to what's going on in the present moment. In this view, life isn't lived in the past or in the future; we're able to engage with our life only right now, in this very moment. Depression can narrow our focus and make us see only the negative things in life; but mindfulness would have us practice remaining open and accepting of everything we see and experience, without then labeling it as good or bad. As an example, if we're depressed, we might think, "I'm such a horrible person. Why would anyone want to talk with me?" If we were to experience this same thought more mindfully, we might say, "I notice I'm having feelings of worthlessness." The feeling is still there; we're not pretending it doesn't exist or that we can magically make it go away. But we're creating some emotional distance between ourselves and that thought, and so it loses some of its power over us.

MINDFUL ACCEPTANCE

In addition to practicing mindful awareness of our experiences, we can also work to accept those experiences as the way life really is right now. When we don't accept the reality of what's going on, that's when we suffer. How many times have you yelled at the universe, "This shouldn't be happening this way"? I often say to my clients that pain is inevitable, but suffering is not; we can reduce our suffering when we accept what's going on in our lives. This is a challenging way of looking at things. But acceptance doesn't mean liking it or approving of it when bad things happen. It doesn't mean becoming helpless or giving up. It just means what it says—accepting what's happening right now. Think about the last time you had car trouble or had a flat tire. Getting angry and thinking "This shouldn't have happened!"

doesn't do anything to fix the problem, and it only makes you feel worse about yourself. As soon as you catch your breath and accept that yes, this tire is flat, or that your "check engine" light is on, you can begin taking action to call for help or do something useful. You don't have to pretend that you're happy; you can still be angry or disappointed! Mindfulness just means noticing the feelings instead of automatically acting on them.

A MINDFULNESS EXERCISE

When it comes to mindfully dealing with depression, I often encourage my clients to let themselves fully feel and experience their emotions, whatever those may be. I often suggest that they imagine that their thoughts are like leaves floating by on a stream or like boxes going by on a conveyor belt (Hayes, Strosahl, and Wilson 2003; Linehan 1993). The goal is to label and notice what you see going by without falling into the stream or getting on the conveyor belt. This can be a very different way of experiencing your thoughts, but again, it helps create emotional distance and prevents you from getting caught up in harmful ways of thinking. There's a world of difference, for instance, between thinking "This sucks...I'm just such a lazy jerk for missing work today...I'm probably going to get fired...I probably deserve it anyway" and the more mindful, less judgmental assessment "I'm noticing that I don't like the feelings I'm having right now...I'm noticing that I'm being judgmental toward myself and calling myself names for missing work...I notice that right now I'm making assumptions about the future and believe things aren't going to go well...and right now, I see that I'm assuming that I deserve those bad things." The latter may seem strange, but notice that it's neutral and non-judgmental, which loosens the grip of the negative thoughts that depression can create.

How Long Will Psychotherapy Last?

There's no one formula for predicting how long therapy will last, but most people begin noticing some improvement in their depressive symptoms after about a month or so in therapy. Typically, therapy will need at least three months to be effective, and some types of therapy should go on for longer. Because there's such a risk of relapse and recurrence with depression, you should talk with your therapist about maintenance treatment—that is, checking in once a month or so for the first year after you're symptom-free. This can help lower the risk of relapse or recurrence and can help you solidify the gains you've made in therapy; I'll cover this further in chapter 9.

MEDICATION

In addition to psychotherapy, medication is a very common treatment for depression. But what can you expect if you consult with your physician or psychiatrist about taking medication? Let's spend some time reviewing what you can expect and what questions you might want to think about before beginning medication treatment.

Maybe the most common misconception that I have to address about antidepressant medications is what they can do. There's no such thing as a pill that makes you happy! Medication won't give anyone a pain-free life; we'd be living in a fantasy land if our lives didn't have any pain. What antidepressant medications can do very well, though, is help your brain generate the right balance of chemicals and neurotransmitters to relieve many of the symptoms of depression. They can help you get back your energy, have more regular sleep, feel like eating again, and overcome the feelings of sluggishness and fatigue that can come along with depression.

What should you expect once you begin taking an antidepressant? You may be surprised to learn that many medications can take up to a month to reach their full efficacy. It's important that you ask your doctor how long it usually takes to notice the benefits of the medication he's recommending. Unfortunately, if the medication you're taking has any side effects, you'll probably notice them sooner than you do the beneficial effects. I always recommend asking your doctor up front what the most common side effects are and how you can manage them effectively during the first few days and weeks of taking the new medication. You should also ask whether there are any side effects that could be considered serious or create an emergency and what you should do if you notice them.

For how long will you have to take medication? Just as with psychotherapy, there are no hard-and-fast rules that apply across the board, but given the risk of relapse or recurrence during the first year, in my experience psychiatrists often recommend staying on antidepressant medication for about a year. This may seem like overkill, but there's a good reason for playing it safe: if someone recovers from depression but then gets depressed again during the first year or so afterward, the odds are that the next depressive episode will be more severe and will last longer. It's very important that you prevent relapse or recurrence, and a longer course of medication can help do just that.

Some patients worry that they'll have to be on medication forever. This usually isn't a realistic worry for most people. After you take medication for the recommended amount of time, your physician or psychiatrist can talk with you about the best way to stop taking it. This often involves weaning you off the medication gradually instead of stopping it all at once. Many modern antidepressants work very well but can lead to very unpleasant side effects if you discontinue them suddenly. Never just guess about the best way to stop taking a medication; always have a conversation with your physician or psychiatrist first.

SHOULD YOU CHOOSE THERAPY, MEDICATION, OR BOTH?

It can be hard to know what kind of treatment to pursue. Medication and therapy will usually both bring symptom relief, and for some people, that's all that matters. These approaches differ, though, in the way that they relieve depressive symptoms. No medication can teach you new coping skills or new ways of thinking about things, so here therapy has the advantage. Conversely, medication can often bring relief from many of the physical symptoms of depression more quickly than talk therapy can.

Talk therapy may work well for you if you're interested in learning more about the ways in which you experience yourself, other people, your emotions, and the events in your life. In your conversations with your therapist, you can come to learn which of these experiences work well for you and which ones might be maladaptive. Even better, therapy provides a confidential and safe relationship in which to try out some new, more effective behaviors. You might have a harder time in talk therapy, however, if you find it difficult to be open about your thoughts and emotions or if you find it extremely difficult to trust other people.

Medication and therapy can work very well together. I sometimes say that medication can do the heavy lifting when it comes to managing the physical and cognitive symptoms of depression, making it easier for you to make the healthy changes that you learn about in therapy. If your physician or psychiatrist suggests one approach but not the other, you should feel free to ask the reason and whether there would be any potential benefit to pursuing both medication and therapy.

SUMMARY

You have a lot of choices when it comes to treating depression, but most of those choices fall under one of two broad headings: taking antidepressant medication or pursuing talk therapy. Either path can provide symptomatic relief, and talk therapy can also help you learn effective coping strategies. Many people choose both and find the combination approach to treatment very helpful. Whether you choose medication, psychotherapy, or both, I want to emphasize that when it comes to depression, either of these treatments is usually a better choice than no treatment. Whichever path you choose, though, it's important for you to be able to track how you're doing over time. In chapter 4, I'll discuss some good ways of seeing how well your treatment is working.

CHAPTER 4

MONITORING YOUR PROGRESS IN TREATMENT

In this chapter, I'll cover how you can monitor your progress from week to week while you're in treatment. I'll also talk about what you can do with that information to help figure out what's working and what's not. Your doctor or therapist might have some additional suggestions for monitoring how you're doing.

FREQUENCY AND METHOD OF MONITORING

When I treat people with depression, frequently I ask them to fill out a brief checklist every week to give me a sense of which symptoms are bothering them and how severe those symptoms are. I usually use the PHQ-9, the checklist that I presented in chapter 2. Using a standardized measure like the PHQ-9 allows my clients and me to track their progress over time. Seeing improvement over time gives us both hope and indicates that we're probably proceeding correctly. When there's a lack of improvement, we can have a conversation about what's not working well. Whether you use a checklist or worksheet or even just have a conversation with your doctor or therapist, it's extremely important that you keep an eye on how you're doing from week to week.

Don't overdo it with monitoring yourself, though. I wouldn't recommend assessing your symptoms more than once a week. Some depression measurements purposely ask about your symptoms over the previous two weeks, instead of a shorter period, in order to make sure that a few really good days or really bad days don't obscure the big picture of your progress over time. It's like weighing yourself every day: the small day-to-day fluctuations will make it hard to see a meaningful long-term pattern; getting a moving average over a longer period gives a more reliable picture. If you're filling out a worksheet or checklist or talking with your health care provider, once a week is generally fine. The exception to this would be if you're having any thoughts of suicide or self-harm, in which case you should talk openly with your therapist about when you should reach out for help urgently. I'll also discuss managing suicidal thoughts in chapter 6.

WHEN SHOULD YOU EXPECT TO SEE SOME CHANGES?

For most people, it takes about a month of being in therapy or taking a medication before they begin to see some improvement. Medications need time to reach effective levels in your system, and life stresses don't change overnight. I like to tell my clients this up front so that they can have realistic expectations about therapy; otherwise, they might feel confused or disappointed when things don't feel too different after a couple of meetings. It's important that you have a candid conversation with your therapist or doctor about when you might expect to see some improvement.

WHAT IF YOU'RE NOT GETTING ANY BETTER?

As I mentioned in chapter 1, research clearly shows that most people who seek treatment for depression get better, and they get better more quickly than people who don't seek treatment. But what if you've sought treatment and things aren't getting better? Sadly, some people will not respond well to the most common treatments for depression. Among depressed people taking medication who aren't also receiving therapy, as many as 30 to 50 percent will not fully respond to their medication (Ruhé et al. 2006). Many clinicians use the term "treatment-resistant depression" to refer to depression that does not respond well to various treatments. Before you assume that you're dealing with treatment-resistant depression, however, it will be important to consider some other possibilities.

Medication Compliance

As many as half of people taking medication for depression will not take it as prescribed after just two months (Eaddy and Regan 2003). There are different reasons for this; some people have mixed feelings about taking medication because they think resorting to medication means that they're weak or that they can't cope by themselves. As a result, they take their medication inconsistently or stop altogether. Having mixed feelings about being depressed and treating it is understandable, but it will be important that you have an honest conversation with your therapist or doctor about what might be stopping you from taking your medication as prescribed.

I sometimes compare taking medication for depression with taking insulin for diabetes; you need to be consistent over the long haul, and there's no need to be ashamed of having an illness. Do you look down on people who take insulin? Probably not, because everyone knows that insulin treatment helps and is an accepted way of treating diabetes. Nobody likes managing a chronic medical condition, but taking care of yourself is not a cause for shame or evidence of weakness. Rather, it shows that you care for yourself enough to do what it takes to treat your illness seriously.

Other people sometimes say that they don't like the side effects of their medication or that it makes them not feel quite like themselves. If your doctor has prescribed medication for you, I would encourage you to ask up front about common side effects and how long they are likely to last. Also, ask how long you should try tolerating any side effects before contacting your doctor. Be aware that in rare cases, some medications can lead to an increase in suicidal thoughts, especially if you're younger than twenty-one. Talk with your doctor up front about making plans if suicidal thoughts become a problem, and follow those plans immediately if they do.

Actively Participating in Therapy

Just as some people have mixed feelings about taking medication, some people have mixed feelings about attending therapy regularly. Being in therapy itself might make them feel less independent, or they might feel that therapy's not for them. Feelings like this aren't a problem—it's how you handle them. As funny as this may sound, if you don't want to go to therapy, it's better to go anyway and talk about why you don't want to be there! Even if this sounds backward, sometimes the reasons you don't want to go to therapy reflect the problems that are keeping you depressed. For instance, maybe you think that what you have to say is worthless and not worth talking about in therapy; but if you went, you might find that this very belief contributes to your depression.

Working these problems out in the safety of your relationship with your therapist can be very important.

Some people don't feel a good connection with their therapist. In most cases, I suggest that you try going to therapy and taking the reasonable risk of addressing these feelings openly with your therapist. You're not going to offend your therapist, and it can be enormously helpful to examine these feelings more closely in therapy. Think about what doesn't feel right about your connection with your therapist; do you find yourself wanting more guidance, for instance? It's okay to be up front about what you want and expect and then ask your therapist for this. Therapists aren't psychic! We need to know what you want, need, and expect, just like anyone else would. Go ahead and tell us!

What if you've tried what I just described, but you still aren't feeling a good connection with your therapist? If you've genuinely tried to work it out, I'd recommend looking for a different therapist. A good therapeutic relationship is one of the best predictors of a successful therapy, and a bad one can get in the way of making good progress. I wouldn't advise switching before you make a good-faith attempt to work things out, though, because your relationship with your therapist can be an important tool for learning healthy interpersonal skills.

Comorbid Diagnoses

Sometimes people don't get better because depression isn't the only problem. Depression rarely occurs in a vacuum. In many cases, depressed people are also dealing with another medical or psychiatric illness at the same time. When two or more diagnoses occur together, they're called comorbid conditions. Chapter 8 is devoted entirely to this topic and will go into detail about the most common comorbid conditions, such as anxiety disorders, substance abuse, and personality disorders.

Ineffective Medication

If you're on medication but it doesn't seem to be working after about a month, it's time to talk with your doctor. And don't despair—there are still numerous routes available with medication. Your doctor might recommend waiting a little longer for your medication to work, changing the dosage, adding another medication to supplement what you're already taking, or even trying a different medication. Most important, do not make any of these changes without speaking with your doctor first. Stopping or changing antidepressant medications suddenly can trigger unwanted effects and is not advisable.

Ineffective Psychotherapy

What if you've been in therapy for over a month and you're not satisfied with how it's going? Again, talking openly is the key. Often when therapy stalls, it's because no clearly defined goal has been established. If you've been monitoring your symptoms like I recommended above, bring in your checklist or worksheet and have an honest talk about what's still bothering you. If you're not sure where therapy's going, it's important that you let your therapist know sooner rather than later so you can both get back on the same page.

But what if you've talked with your therapist and you're still not satisfied with the progress you're seeing in therapy? Ask yourself these questions:

- What are my goals in therapy, and are we focusing on them enough when we meet?

- Does my therapist seem to understand me and my goals for therapy?

- Do I understand where therapy is headed, or does it just seem to be drifting right now?

- Do I understand what style of therapy we're using?

About this last point: recall from chapter 3 that there are numerous kinds of therapy, many of which are effective treatments for depression. We know from research that certain types of therapy are empirically proven to work well with depression, such as cognitive therapy, interpersonal therapy, and psychodynamic psychotherapy. If your therapist recommends or uses a different type of therapy, this doesn't necessarily mean that her style of therapy is ineffective, but it does mean it's okay to ask why she believes her style of therapy should help treat depression. Competent therapists won't get defensive or angry if you ask them about this; they should be able to explain what they're thinking and recommending without using any complicated language or psychological jargon. If you don't understand where your therapist is coming from, it's important that you bring this up quickly.

What If Nothing Else Works?

If a depressive episode becomes severe for a long enough time, or if the depressed person becomes imminently suicidal, sometimes hospitalization makes sense. Hospitalization usually doesn't provide any special kind of treatment for depression apart from those mentioned so far, but it does provide safety, structure, and a simpler environment while the depressed person works on getting better. Some hospitals do offer specialized treatments for people with depression or other mood disorders, such as educational groups, intensive psychotherapy, and close medication management. If you think you may benefit from specialized services like these, check with your therapist or psychiatrist to see whether there is any benefit to a partial or full hospitalization.

The very small number of people who do not respond to any conventional treatment for depression might benefit from electroconvulsive therapy (ECT). If this term immediately conjures up images from horror movies, where helpless patients are tied down and tortured with shocks by sadistic doctors, be assured that the reality is much different. Very few depressed people ever have to resort to ECT, but for those who do, it often provides relief from chronic severe depression. In modern ECT, patients are given a sedative; while they're asleep, a small amount of electric current—about the same amount needed to power a light bulb—is briefly passed through one or both halves of the patient's brain through electrodes placed on the head. This triggers a seizure, but the sedatives prevent full-on convulsions. During the seizure, the patient's brain releases numerous chemicals that, over time, appear to help some people with severe depression.

How to Talk with Your Doctors If You're Not Improving

I've been saying consistently that it's important for you to talk with your doctor or therapist if you're not improving or you're not satisfied with how your treatment is progressing, but sometimes this can be harder than it sounds. Some people don't feel comfortable asserting themselves at all, much less to someone in a position of authority. Doctors hold places of special respect in most cultures, and it can feel intimidating to talk directly with physicians or therapists about your problems with the treatment they prescribe. Because good communication is so important, though, let's spend a little time talking about how you might bring up your concerns.

Before speaking with your doctor, you should be clear in your own head about what you want your doctor to know and what questions you have regarding how to proceed. I'd recommend taking some time to write down your concerns, to help you organize your thoughts. For instance, you might feel like the medication you were prescribed is not helping or has unwanted side effects. Or you might feel that you're not meeting often enough to have the time to address all the concerns that you believe are maintaining your depressed mood. Whatever the concerns are, it's a good idea to write them down and bring these notes with you to your next meeting with your doctor or therapist.

Next, it's very important that you think about what you want to be different. Perhaps your medication is making you overly tired, and you need this to stop; or perhaps you feel like your doctor doesn't understand just how hopeless or depressed you really feel, and you want her to appreciate this more. Being clear about what you want to change will help you remember that you're voicing your legitimate needs and not just complaining.

How can you bring up your concerns? I'd recommend bringing them up at the beginning of your appointment. Most sessions begin with the therapist or doctor checking in about how things have been going since you last met, so this is an ideal time. Plus, the longer the session goes on, the more you're going to be thinking about the concerns that you haven't brought up yet—so go ahead and mention them early. Even though it might feel awkward at first, you'll feel better knowing that you're taking your problems seriously enough to bring them up. And remember, doctors aren't psychic! They won't know what you're concerned about unless you tell them.

SUMMARY

Most people who seek treatment for depression should see some improvement within about a month of beginning treatment. I recommend using a structured way of tracking your progress over time so that you and your health care provider can judge which symptoms are improving and which ones aren't. When you don't find relief from depressive symptoms as quickly as you had expected, there could be several explanations, ranging from comorbid conditions to the treatment being ineffective. You should talk with your doctor or therapist about what to do when treatment doesn't seem to be working. Open, honest communication is important and can help you have realistic expectations for improvement.

Once you're in the habit of monitoring your progress in treatment, what else can you do to take care of yourself? In chapter 5, I'll focus on managing your symptoms of depression.

CHAPTER 5

MANAGING YOUR SYMPTOMS

For this chapter, we're going to focus on the most common symptoms of depression and how you can manage them while you're getting treatment. Remember, these strategies are ideas for symptom management, not symptom removal. There's no way to suddenly snap out of a sad mood or to magically regain interest in activities and relationships when you've been feeling detached and distant. Just remember that even though your depressive symptoms can't disappear overnight, they should diminish over time with proper treatment.

THE BIG PICTURE OF SYMPTOM MANAGEMENT

There may be a certain amount of "going through the motions" for a while as you do the things you normally do, but without your normal enthusiasm. It doesn't work to wait for your mood or motivation to improve before doing anything, and in fact, isolating yourself from your normal activities and your friends, family, and peers will actually make your depression worse. What you'll find is that motivation and an improved mood often follow taking action that benefits you. I want to focus, then, on what you can do to take some healthy action and avoid getting stuck.

LOW ENERGY AND FATIGUE

I'm grouping low energy and fatigue together because they combine to make you feel unable to do the things you used to do. They are some of the most challenging symptoms to manage because there's no way to quickly overcome them, and they can affect many areas of your life. What are some of the ways in which these problems have affected you? Have you had trouble getting up in time for work or school? Have you felt too tired to go out with friends, or have you felt unable to meet some of your social obligations? This is normal, though frustrating. One of the physical symptoms of depression is that you have less energy than you used to, which can combine with negative views of yourself to create a vicious circle: when you fall behind in your daily routine, it's easy to feel bad, guilty, or even hopeless about getting caught up, making it even easier to not want to try again. You can remind yourself that it's very important for you to prevent this cycle from taking hold or to break out of it if it already has. Your goal isn't to somehow pretend you're not fatigued, or to try to push through your tiredness with superhuman effort; it's to do the best you can with the energy you have and to feel satisfied that you're doing everything you can. I'll talk later in this chapter about the balance between doing what you can and temporarily lowering your expectations for yourself.

When you're fatigued or have low energy, you're of course not going to do everything you used to be able to do. It's important, then, to spend your energy on the things that are most important to you and then accept that lower-priority things will just have to wait. Whenever possible, structure your day to accommodate your symptoms. This might mean leaving yourself time for a nap if you can't stay awake, or it might mean making sure that you do more challenging work earlier in the day while you still have the energy.

Charting Your Symptoms

It can help to keep a simple chart of your energy level in the morning, afternoon, and evening so that you can see whether you're most fatigued at a certain time and then plan accordingly. I recommend a chart of your energy, sleep, and mood levels like the one that follows so that you can learn more about your pattern of symptoms and about the effect of various activities. Jot down your ratings of your energy, sleep, and mood for each day of the week. You can rate your energy and mood on a scale from 1 to 10, with 1 representing extremely low energy or mood and 10 representing extremely high energy or mood. For your sleep, write down how many hours of sleep you got the previous night. Finally, in the column marked "Activities," jot down any particular activities that you tried that day. Over time, this can help you learn which activities seem to help your mood and energy and which ones don't seem to help as much. This kind of chart is useful because it's quick, doesn't require much effort, and helps you notice patterns over time. If you miss a day, that's okay; just try to resume filling out your chart as soon as you can. You might also want to take your chart to your mental health provider because it could be very useful to him in understanding what makes you feel better and what makes you feel worse.

Mood, Energy, Sleep, and Activity Tracking

	Energy (1–10)	Hours of sleep	Mood (1–10)	Activities
Monday Morning Midday Evening				

Tuesday Morning Midday Evening				
Wednesday Morning Midday Evening				
Thursday Morning Midday Evening				
Friday Morning Midday Evening				
Saturday Morning Midday Evening				
Sunday Morning Midday Evening				

LOSS OF INTEREST AND SOCIAL ISOLATION

What about a lack of interest in activities that used to interest you? Just as with a sad mood, there's no way to "snap out of it" when you're not feeling very interested in the things you used to enjoy. It's easy to feel bored or to believe that it's not worth it to get involved with something when you're depressed. Worse, staying at home or in your room for long periods can trigger a spiral of feeling useless that makes you want to isolate yourself even more. It's very important, then, to find ways of staying active so that you don't feel stagnant.

Staying Active

The good news is that once you begin making an effort to get involved in outside activities, it can increase your motivation to continue doing so. Psychologists sometimes use the term "behavioral activation" to refer to ways of taking effective action and staying involved. To make use of these principles, keep a list of some daily activities that you want to try or that you used to do, and note how doing them now affects your mood. If you find that certain activities have a positive effect on your mood, continue building those activities into your day when possible—and stick with them! Here are some ideas:

- Going for a walk

- Cooking a meal for yourself or others

- Getting outside instead of staying indoors

- Calling a friend

- Going to the grocery store

- Going to the gym or an exercise class

- Inviting a friend over for coffee

- Yoga, meditation, swimming, or other healthy activities

If you find that you're unable to stick to those goals, you might need to break them down into smaller steps that are easier to accomplish. For instance, if you feel overwhelmed at the idea of going to the gym, you could encourage yourself to do one step at a time: walk to the car; drive to the gym; change clothes; exercise; shower; change clothes; and drive home. Seeing the smaller steps can make larger tasks feel more reasonable and less overwhelming.

Maintaining Relationships

Social isolation, like loss of interest, can be hard to deal with because when you're depressed, sometimes the last thing you want to do is be around other people. Social contact might seem pointless, frustrating, or even annoying. Just as with loss of interest, though, it's important that you make reasonable social goals and then stick to them. Maybe you don't feel like having company or going to a party, but setting a smaller goal like meeting a friend for a short coffee break at least once a week can help you be around other people and avoid the trap of isolation and loneliness. You don't have to pressure yourself for these social engagements to be anything ambitious; just making the effort to be around other people can be an important start. The tracking strategy above can work well in your relationships, too: Make a list of the important people in your life and then keep track of how your time spent with them or talking with them affects your mood. Do you need to be spending more time with certain people? Less? It's important that you have a good grasp on how your relationships affect your mood and then act accordingly to improve the situations that aren't working and to make the most of the ones that are.

Keeping a Consistent Schedule

When you're less interested in your usual routines, I encourage you to keep to a regular schedule as much as possible. Consistency from day to day is very important when you're depressed—this doesn't mean creating boredom or monotony, but it does mean keeping a reliable routine. When you're depressed is never a good time to "wing it" or leave your days completely unstructured, because you run the risk of drifting aimlessly. Of course, this is easier said than done; when you're depressed, your heart just isn't into planning or staying active. But by keeping to regular activities like consistent mealtimes, a bedtime, and other routines, you can trust that you're doing something important and good for yourself and preventing yourself from drifting and feeling aimless.

SAD MOODS

Feeling sad or down is one of the most difficult depressive symptoms to manage, simply because there's no way to just snap out of it. I want to suggest three broad strategies for coping with a sad mood. You can experiment with them to see which one works best for you.

Distracting Yourself

First, for short periods, there's nothing wrong with distracting yourself. Talking with a friend, watching a movie, or even driving around for a while can be fine ways of temporarily getting your mind off being sad. I don't recommend making this your primary way of coping, because if you're distracting yourself too much for long periods, you might be less motivated to focus on your treatment goals. For the short run, though, distraction can be an excellent strategy.

Accepting Your Sadness

Second, try accepting your sadness as the way you're feeling right now. Recall from chapter 3 that this doesn't mean giving up; it just means being honest about your current mood. Acceptance frees you up to do something about your mood instead of getting caught up in thoughts like "It's not fair that I have to deal with this" (Hayes, Strosahl, and Wilson 2003).

Challenging Negative Thoughts

Finally, drawing from the principles of cognitive therapy, it's sometimes useful to identify the particular thoughts you're having that are making you feel sad. For instance, you might find yourself thinking, "I'm so lazy; I've missed three days of work this week," or "Why bother calling anyone? Nobody would want to talk with me anyway." Depression makes you tend to think in extremes, and challenging these extreme thoughts when they arrive can be important. When you find yourself dwelling on an extreme negative thought, notice it and check out the evidence for it. Which is more likely: that an extreme negative belief is true or that the depression has made your thinking more extreme and negative? Reminding yourself of this won't make negative thoughts disappear, but it can buy you some emotional distance from them.

SLEEP DISTURBANCES

People with depression very commonly have disturbed sleep. Most people with depression sleep less than they used to, but some find themselves oversleeping and having little incentive to get out of bed. I'll talk about managing each of these problems.

Strategies for Managing Insomnia

It's common for someone who is depressed to have insomnia, which can mean trouble falling asleep, unwanted waking in the middle of sleep, or waking up earlier than intended. If you have trouble falling asleep or if you wake up and can't get back to sleep within fifteen to twenty minutes, get out of bed for a while and do something low-key, such as reading or taking a warm bath. Return to bed after a while and wait for sleep again, but remember that you can't force it. If you wake up an hour or less earlier than you intended to, it's best to go ahead and get out of bed. Lying in bed wishing you could sleep is unlikely to work well, and it may just make you frustrated.

I said earlier in this chapter that keeping a consistent schedule, including your sleep schedule, is important. Because depression can alter your sleep patterns significantly, it can be difficult to keep to a regular sleep schedule. You might not be able to control what time you fall asleep, but you do have a little more control over what time you get out of bed. For this reason, I recommend setting an alarm for around the same time each day and then doing your best to get out of bed when it goes off. Even if you're still tired, it can pay to go ahead and get out of bed. One reason is that you're more likely to be tired at the end of your day and get better quality sleep. Also, by getting out of bed, you avoid the trap of accidentally going back to sleep and missing much of your day. Worse, staying in bed for too long can get your sleep *out of phase*, meaning that you're more prone to sleep during the day and be awake at night. It's best to keep to a regular schedule; it will help your body know what to expect and will give you some consistency and stability in your day.

What about naps? Short naps of up to half an hour are sometimes helpful, but when you're recovering from depression, I usually discourage them because they create an opportunity to oversleep. Realistically, of course, giving up naps isn't always possible; if you do take a nap, be sure to set an alarm for thirty minutes, and don't take more than one nap per day.

I often recommend to my clients with depression that they try some form of light exercise in the early evenings. Not only does the exercise involve healthy movement and activity, but it will help you sleep better that night, even if it's just a light walk.

Be sure to avoid alcohol, caffeine, and big meals right before bed. Watching your alcohol intake is a good idea in general when you're recovering from depression, of course, but if you do drink, don't do it in the few hours right before you go to bed. Your body treats alcohol like any other food, and digesting lots of food can actually interfere with falling asleep. Caffeine, of course, is a stimulant and can make it harder to fall asleep if you drink it too close to bedtime. Try to cut out caffeine for at least four hours before bedtime—and even earlier, if possible.

For my clients with insomnia, I always remind them not to use their beds for anything other than sleep and sex. In other words, don't watch TV or read in bed; you can wind up conditioning yourself to be paying attention in bed rather than resting (Hirshkowitz, Moore, and Minhoto 1997). If you want to read or watch TV, be sure to get out of bed while you do it.

Strategies for Dealing with Sleeping Too Much

Most depressed people will deal with some form of insomnia, but some will sleep too much—also called *hypersomnia*.

Hypersomnia is extremely frustrating: you feel like you just can't get enough sleep, so you sleep some more, only to find that it wasn't refreshing or restful. Dealing with hypersomnia is much easier said than done, but it can be managed. I recommend getting out of bed, even if it's difficult, once you wake up after sleeping for eight hours. Your may feel tired at that point, but staying in bed further will generally not help and may represent more of a wish to withdraw from the world than a genuine need to sleep (White and Mitler 1997). By staying in bed, you inadvertently miss out on opportunities to reestablish your usual routine. You can also accidentally fuel guilty feelings when you stay in bed too long. Worse, any additional sleep you get is unlikely to leave you any more refreshed. It's very helpful to set an alarm or even ask a friend to call you and make sure you're out of bed by a certain time.

If Sleep Problems Persist

Finally, if any sleep problem persists or feels too difficult to manage, talk with your physician or psychiatrist. Some sleep problems may reflect a sleep disorder instead of a depressive symptom and might require separate treatment. As one example, sleep apnea is a sleep disorder in which a person stops breathing for short periods while asleep, leaving him oxygen-starved and exhausted the next day. Also, some antidepressant medications can inadvertently disrupt your sleep, so be sure to let your psychiatrist know if you're having any problem sleeping.

CHANGES IN APPETITE

Many depressed people don't feel like eating. If they do, they might eat much less than usual, causing them to lose weight. Food might just not seem as appetizing to you anymore, and cooking for yourself might feel like it takes too much effort. Sadly, poor appetite can worsen the depressive episode directly, by robbing the body of nutrients it needs to stay healthy, and indirectly because missing meals can mean missing out on daily structure and opportunities for social contact.

Eating Regularly and Healthily

Since you do have to eat, though, let's focus on how you can do it in a way that meets your body's needs. When you do sit down to eat, what should you have? Since you're probably eating more for function than for fun when you're depressed, be sure to give your body the nutrition it needs while you're recovering. In 2009, Sánchez-Villegas and colleagues found that diets high in legumes, fruits, and vegetables and low in meats and dairy appeared to have a protective effect against depression. Healthy meals like these not only meet your body's nutritional needs, but also give you a reason to add some activity to your routine by going to the grocery store or doing some light cooking for yourself.

Try to keep your regular mealtimes, even when you don't feel like it. Regular mealtimes can help bring some structure to your day. Try eating with others when you feel up to it so that you can have opportunities for social contact. If you've been dealing with low energy, breakfast will be particularly important.

Coping with Overeating

Some depressed people go to the other extreme and begin overeating. Good food can comfort us when we feel down, and when we're depressed, it's natural to need lots of comfort. It's very common to crave large amounts of carbohydrates, particularly sugars, and it's easy to overdo it by relying on the convenience of processed foods. But remember that even though carb binges may make you feel better temporarily, they can worsen feelings of lethargy and depression once the burst of energy wears off and leaves you with a "carb crash."

If you're struggling with overeating when you're depressed, you might want to begin writing down how you're feeling when you're tempted to eat. Many people who do this find that they're eating not because they're hungry but because they're bored or dealing with another unpleasant emotion. Learning what your triggers are for eating won't make the cravings go away, but it will give you a chance to think of some ways of coping with those feelings that don't necessarily involve food.

When you do eat, practice the mindfulness skills I mentioned earlier. Instead of eating quickly and mechanically, slow down and pay attention to the experience of eating. What's the texture of the food in your mouth? What does it taste like? Can you bring your full attention to the act of eating instead of thinking about other things? You'll get more satisfaction from your meals this way, and you'll be much more aware of what you're taking in.

GUILT

You may have heard depression described as "anger turned inward." Even though this is an oversimplification, many people with depression do find it easier to blame themselves for life's problems instead of feeling compassion for themselves.

Having Compassion for Yourself

When you're depressed, self-compassion is extremely important. When you're depressed, you're sick, and being angry with people for being sick just doesn't accomplish much. We don't get mad at ourselves for having the flu or a kidney infection, because we know that we didn't cause the problem and that our job is to get better, not to feel bad about ourselves. It's no different with depression. Some people with depression worry that if they're kind to themselves instead of harsh, then they'll somehow feel even lazier or lose their motivation to get better. I often suggest that this belief is actually making them feel worse. Drill sergeants rarely make effective therapists!

Accepting Support

People with depression often worry that they're being a burden on their friends and family. You may even have worried that you're being frustrating or annoying by asking others for help. But think about it like this: You're doing your part. When you're sick, you have a responsibility to get treatment and work on getting better—and it's socially acceptable to ask for more support. When you have the flu, you do your part by staying home from work, resting, and taking care of yourself; you probably wouldn't feel guilty for asking someone to bring you a box of tissues. It's no different with depression.

PROBLEMS WITH CONCENTRATING AND MAKING DECISIONS

Isn't it frustrating to misplace your keys or go to the grocery store and forget what you needed? We've all had normal lapses in memory and concentration, but when we're depressed, they can be even more common. I've even had some clients refer to it as "brain fog" because it can be so debilitating. Even if you think you don't need to, it can be a good idea to make more lists to remind yourself of things while you're working on getting better. It's just a temporary measure until you're better able to concentrate and focus. If you have a computer or cell phone that allows you to set periodic alarms or reminders for yourself, try using them to remind you of some tasks or responsibilities like ones you may have recently forgotten. Also, following the sleep management tips above can help ensure that you're at your best mentally.

What if you're feeling so indecisive that it's hard to know what to do next? Coping with indecision is frustrating. Remind yourself that your goal is not to figure out the perfect decision. Instead, just try to make good enough decisions in the direction of keeping yourself active and socially engaged. When you're depressed, it's not the best time to make major life decisions, but if you're really stuck, consider asking someone you trust for his perspective. Finally, if you're feeling paralyzed by a decision, ask yourself whether it's more important to spend more time on it or to make a choice in the name of getting yourself unstuck.

TEMPORARILY ADJUSTING YOUR EXPECTATIONS

Many of the symptoms of depression can make it more difficult to work, study, read, or be engaged in any activity. Part of managing your symptoms effectively is temporarily adjusting your expectations for yourself. It simply doesn't make sense to expect yourself to be at 100 percent with the hundred-pound weight of depression on your back. There's nothing noble about not asking for the help you need, and I encourage you to be an advocate for yourself. If you had a cast on your leg and were walking with crutches, people would see that you needed some help and would open doors for you; but because depression isn't visible to others in the same way, it becomes especially important that you be open about the life changes you need while you're recovering. Remember: people won't know what you need unless you let them know—so tell them! I'll focus on some strategies for doing this in chapter 7.

SUMMARY

Even though depressive symptoms don't go away overnight, there are many strategies you can use to cope with them and manage them while you're recovering. What's important is to be active in caring for yourself, even if you don't initially feel like it. Staying active and engaged in caring for yourself can help fight off sluggishness and apathy. Experiment with these suggestions to find out which ones work for you, and be sure to talk with your therapist or psychiatrist to see whether what you're doing is compatible with your treatment plan. Perhaps most importantly, be consistent—change doesn't happen overnight, and it's important that you stick with the strategies that are working for you. In the next chapter, I'll focus on a particular kind of symptom management: dealing with suicidal thoughts.

CHAPTER 6

MANAGING SUICIDAL THOUGHTS

When discussing symptom management with depression, one symptom is serious enough to warrant special attention—thoughts of suicide. Discussing the risk for suicide may seem frightening or intimidating at first, but it's necessary. Depression takes an enormous toll, but suicidal thinking can make it turn deadly. I've divided this chapter into two main sections—the first for you if you're depressed, and the second for you to review with the important people in your life so they can help you manage any thoughts of suicide.

Tragically, suicide is a real risk among people with depression. Obviously, most people who have depression don't kill themselves, but most suicide victims were dealing with a mental illness at the time—usually depression. Why is there a relationship between depression and suicide? What is it about this illness that can make people despair enough to overcome their most basic instinct: to survive? In large part, it's because depression can lead to intense feelings of hopelessness, or the belief that things will never get better (Beck 1986). Combine this belief with feelings of guilt and self-criticism, a loss of social supports, and a loss of pleasure and other reasons to live, and you can begin to understand why some people reach the conclusion that their life is not worth living. It's not that they want to die as much as they lose hope and don't see any other way to stop hurting (Jobes 2006). The good news is that these thoughts and feelings begin to improve as the depression remits, so seeking treatment for depression is extremely important in order to lessen the risk.

FOR THOSE WHO ARE FEELING SUICIDAL

"Feeling suicidal" can refer to a wide variety of thoughts, feelings, and actions. Picture a spectrum ranging from less severe to more severe. At the less severe end of the continuum, you may have vague thoughts of wanting to disappear or wishing that your pain would quickly go away. As these thoughts take root over time, the thoughts get darker: you might wonder whether anyone would miss you if you were dead or whether the world would be better off without you. With enough time, this can give way to actually making preparations, such as researching ways to die, stockpiling pills, or purchasing a gun. Finally, at the riskiest end of the spectrum, there is the intent to die. Intent to die may be planned, or it may arise impulsively under the influence of drugs or alcohol. So it's important when we talk about suicidal thoughts and actions to be specific about how far you've gotten on this spectrum. Let's focus, then, on different interventions you can use at various stages of severity.

If you're primarily having thoughts about suicide, but you haven't made plans or have no intention of actually doing it, there's time to reduce the risk and increase your protective factors—and though you should make plans to manage the suicidal thoughts, your primary focus at this point should be on treating the depression. The depressive episode is likely the underlying cause of the suicidal thoughts, and your focus should remain on getting treatment for it. It's very important that you be honest with your therapist, psychiatrist, or physician about any thoughts of dying or suicide at this point, no matter how vague or abstract. This is so she can help you put a safety plan in place now, while the risk is lower. Talking about your suicidal thoughts with someone you trust doesn't make your thoughts worse—it helps you cope with them.

There may be times when it doesn't feel safe to let someone know about your suicidal thoughts. Think twice about opening up to people who tend to overreact, who cannot respect your privacy, or whom you don't know very well, because you don't want them to inadvertently make things worse. Try to find someone you believe will not overreact but who will still take you seriously.

If you cannot think of anyone, consider calling one of the national suicide hotlines listed below.

If you've gone so far as thinking about how you would die, or making plans for how you would kill yourself, the situation is very serious. It may even seem pointless to read about strategies for saving your life because you may feel committed to dying—but there's still reason to hope. We know from interviews with people who unsuccessfully tried to commit suicide that they were usually ambivalent about dying—that is, once they had taken action, such as ingesting pills or jumping off a bridge, they often immediately regretted it. While there's still part of you that's open to receiving help, it's important for you to let someone know now that you're not feeling safe. If you have a friend, family member, or counselor whom you trust, now is the time to let them know. If you're in treatment, you need to let your provider know as soon as possible if you've hit the point of making suicidal plans. And if you have any concern that you cannot control your actions, it's time to call 911 or go to the hospital.

If you've gotten to the point of being ready to take some kind of action to die, the situation is critical. You may have made a decision to die, but there may be some small part of you that isn't sure or that wants to hold on to life. This is a life-or-death emergency, and you should call 911 or get to a hospital immediately. If for some reason this isn't possible, you can call a national suicide hotline at 1-800-SUICIDE (1-800-784-2433) or 1-800-273-TALK (1-800-273-8255). These hotlines are staffed by trained counselors who can talk with you and help you think of ways to cope.

Decreasing Risk

One important strategy in managing suicidal thoughts is to reduce your risk for suicide. Important steps include:

- **Reducing impulsivity by not taking drugs or alcohol.** If you've had any suicidal thoughts, it can be very smart to limit your access to these substances by either taking them out of your home or temporarily giving them to a friend.

- **Limiting access to means of suicide, such as firearms, pills, and high places.** Having access to a gun in your home while you're dealing with suicidal thoughts can be lethal; make sure that any guns are safely stored away, or—even better—find a way to temporarily get them off the premises. If you have access to lethal amounts of medication, talk with a friend or family member about taking temporary custody of your medication so that you don't have access in a moment of despair or impulsivity. I'll talk shortly about ways of enlisting others' help in a useful way without unnecessarily scaring or panicking them.

- **Making sure that you're actively participating in your treatment for depression.** Stopping your therapy or medication can trigger a crisis; talk about it with your therapist, psychiatrist, or physician first. Don't make a rash decision about your treatment.

Increasing Protective Factors

In addition to reducing risks, there are some things you can do to increase your protection against suicide. Some important factors are:

- **Making sure you have timely access to good treatment for depression.** This means making sure your health insurance doesn't lapse; knowing when your next appointment is and making sure transportation is not a problem; making sure that you refill any prescription well in advance of running out of medication; and knowing how to reach your provider in case of an emergency.

- **Being in regular social contact with friends and family members.** Even if you don't feel 100 percent like yourself, having regular social contact can reduce feelings of isolation, avoidance, and loneliness. Having family and social support can be critical, so find a way of letting others know that you want to spend more time with them.

- **Reminding yourself of your personal philosophy of life and your reasons for wanting to live.** Some people have cultural, religious, or philosophical beliefs that can help protect them against suicide. Make the effort to check in with yourself and review your reasons for valuing life and why you believe it's worth living. Even if those reasons aren't as strong as they used to be, it's important that you find what's still meaningful to you and what you can still hold on to.

Making a Safety Plan

One important thing you can do to manage suicidal thoughts is make a specific safety plan and know when it's time to put it into action. Let's take a look at what a good safety plan looks like.

First, where should you go? Is there a place where you feel safer, like home or a friend's house? Have the thoughts become so intense that you need to go to the hospital? If you need to go somewhere, let a friend or family member know where you're going so the people close to you don't get unnecessarily worried.

Second, whom should you call or talk with? Should you call your therapist, and if so, what plans do you have for reaching her? If another person or other people are involved in your emergency plan, be sure to talk with them about it in advance so they can be aware and on board with being part of your plan. Whom can you reach out to if it's late at night? Make sure you have that person's contact information available; you don't want to wait until you're in a crisis to find out that you don't have your friend's new number entered correctly in your cell phone.

How to Let Others Know You Need Help

How can you talk with others about the fact that you've been having thoughts of suicide? Having friends, family, and providers on board can help make managing those thoughts so much easier, but it can be hard to know how to start the conversation. You need to think carefully about:

1. Why you want a particular person to know you've been having suicidal thoughts;

2. What you want and need from that person; and

3. How you can best communicate those needs to this person without making her feel overly responsible for your life.

If you want to talk with someone because you want her emotional support, let her know up front that you're getting treatment, that you want her to be a friend, and that you're not expecting her to be a therapist. This will help her focus on supporting you instead of taking on impossible or unnecessary responsibilities. Let her know that you just need her to listen and to understand what you're going through.

If you need some help from someone because you're not sure you can currently manage your suicidal thoughts by yourself, the situation is urgent. Consider saying something like "I need to talk with you because I've been dealing with depression for a while now. It's gotten to the point where I've even been having some thoughts of dying recently, and I'm scared. I'm not sure that I can manage these thoughts on my own anymore, and I'd like you to (contact my therapist / take me to the hospital / or whatever else you need). I'm doing everything I can to manage these thoughts, but I'm not sure I can do it by myself anymore."

Even when you involve others, ultimately you're responsible for protecting yourself when you're suicidal. There's a world of·

difference between asking for others' help and threatening them. Of course, it's not acceptable to use suicidal thoughts to threaten or blackmail someone into doing what you want. Not only is this unfair and damaging to others, but it is the exact opposite of one of the goals of treatment—taking responsibility for your life.

Some people are afraid to disclose suicidal thoughts to their therapist or psychiatrist because they're afraid that they'll be forcibly hospitalized or trigger some kind of emergency. It doesn't work this way; what talking about suicide with your doctor or therapist does trigger is a conversation. Your therapist will talk with you about what your thoughts have been, how intense they are, and how well you're managing them. If the thoughts are so intense that there's a real risk of you acting on them, your therapist will talk with you about how you can work together to ensure your safety. This might include being evaluated at a hospital, but it's only in the most serious situations that someone can be hospitalized involuntarily.

FOR FRIENDS AND FAMILY OF SOMEONE DEALING WITH SUICIDALITY

This section is intended for friends and family of someone who may be depressed and dealing with suicidal thoughts. It can be frightening and emotionally difficult to talk openly about suicide, but sadly, it's a very real risk for many people who are diagnosed with depression. It's important, then, to familiarize yourself with the risk factors and warning signs for suicide and to know how you can be supportive and helpful.

One of the most destructive myths about suicide is that if you ask someone whether she's suicidal, then she'll be more likely to kill herself. Actually, exactly the opposite is true. When you can show that you're comfortable asking someone directly whether she's been struggling with thoughts of suicide, you show that you're taking that person seriously and that you care enough to ask. The suicidal person is not going to get any ideas she hasn't already had, and she is most likely to feel relief that someone is taking her seriously enough to ask the hard questions. If you're concerned, always ask. You're not going to make it worse, and you could help save the life of someone you care about.

Risk Factors and Warning Signs for Suicide

When you're talking with someone who's depressed and has suicidal thoughts, it's important that you educate yourself about the risk factors and warning signs for suicide. Think about risk factors as conditions that increase the eventual likelihood of suicide in the long run, and think of warning signs as clues that someone is imminently at risk for suicide.

What are some long-term risk factors for suicide? These factors don't cause suicide as much as lower the barriers to it.

- Depression or another psychiatric diagnosis

- Access to a lethal means of suicide, especially firearms

- A history of prior suicide attempts or actions (Most people who die by suicide have made at least one prior attempt.)

- Interpersonal isolation

- Exposure to the suicidal behavior of others

- Having been in jail, even briefly

Even though anyone can commit suicide, older white males are the group at greatest risk.

What are some of the more immediate warning signs for suicide? Some common ones are listed below—if you spot any one of these, it should lead you to ask immediately whether the person is thinking of dying.

- Talking about death, dying, or suicide, even indirectly

- Writing suicide notes, giving away possessions, or updating one's will for no apparent reason

- A sudden, dramatic lift in spirits after having been depressed (This may sound contradictory, but most improvement in depression is gradual. A sudden, dramatic improvement in mood can mean that the depressed person has made the decision to die and is relieved by that decision.)

- Abusing alcohol or drugs, because this can lead to impulsive actions

- A sudden, significant change in the person's usual functioning (Sudden impairment at work or school, or a sudden change in personal grooming or appearance, should be cause for concern.)

- A recent significant loss, such as a breakup; the death of a friend, family member, or pet; or losing one's job

What You Can Do

When helping a friend who is suicidal, you need to remember your role and your limits. You're there to be supportive and encouraging, not to be the suicidal person's therapist. You can't magically fix the situation, but you can help play a role in helping the suicidal person reduce her risk. Here are some of the things that you can do:

- Don't be afraid to ask her directly about suicide. Remember that you will not give her any ideas by asking. If you're not sure what to say, just be honest and direct: for example, "Look, I'm really concerned by everything you're telling me. It's making me wonder whether things have gotten so bad that you've been thinking about ending your life. Are you?"

- Ask how intense and how pressing the suicidal thoughts are. The more intense and pressing the thoughts, the more serious the situation is, and the quicker you should involve the police or get the person to a hospital. If the situation is less intense—that is, if the person says she does not have any intent of acting on those thoughts, and she can demonstrate that she is actively working to manage them—you have time and options. This might include asking to consult with the person's therapist, doctor, or psychiatrist.

- Just being there for the person and being open, caring, and nonjudgmental is itself extremely helpful and can reduce a person's suicide risk. Listen to what she has to say, even if you see things differently. You don't have to have just the right thing to say. Just be real and express your care and concern for her well-being and safety.

- Remain realistically hopeful and optimistic. This doesn't mean making vague promises that everything will be all right, but it does mean reminding the suicidal person that she is feeling this way because she's depressed and that her depression is treatable. Support her in her treatment and her efforts to get better.

- Try to decrease the suicidal person's anxiety. The risk for suicide is higher when people are anxious and agitated, because they're more likely to do something impulsive to relieve their immediate suffering. You might offer to walk with the suicidal person to a place that's quiet or relaxing so you can talk, or you might offer to accompany her somewhere away from a stressful situation. Or you could ask whether the suicidal person would like to do something together to take her mind off her pain for a while. This should not include using alcohol or drugs, of course, but short-term distractions can be a fine way of temporarily reducing anxiety and distress.

- Don't try to fix the problem. You can be most helpful by being a warm, empathic listener. Barraging a suicidal person with endless questions of "Have you tried this yet?" will probably only frustrate her. Instead, help her think through short-term plans for reducing her immediate distress, staying active and involved with her life, and staying engaged with her treatment.

- Follow up! Supporting someone who has suicidal thoughts is an ongoing process, and you should check in from time to time to make sure she is getting the ongoing help and treatment she needs. At the same time, resist the temptation to "watch her like a hawk." If you're so worried about someone that you feel you need to monitor her constantly, either you may be overly worried or the person may need a higher level of care than she's currently getting. Check out your concerns with the depressed person and see whether it makes sense to consult with her provider about her level of care.

- Be sure to take care of yourself. Supporting someone who is suicidal can be difficult and emotionally draining; be sure that you have your own outlets and supports and that you're meeting your own needs as well. If you're spending excessive amounts of time supporting someone who is suicidal, or if you feel that you're being asked to take on too much of an active role in her life, work with that person to reevaluate your place in her safety plan. She may inadvertently be expecting too much from you.

What Not to Do

In your role as a friend or support for someone who may be struggling with suicidal thoughts, there are some things that you should not do because they can make the situation worse. I'll list some common errors so you can be aware of things that are unlikely to help.

- Don't ignore or downplay the person's talk of suicide. Always take the threat seriously. Most people who commit suicide communicate their intentions beforehand; never dismiss their distress as "just talk."

- Similarly, don't dismiss talk of suicide as "just wanting attention." Suicidal crises require attention, and overlooking the warning signs can be fatal.

- At the same time, don't overreact. If someone tells you that she's having some vague thoughts of dying but has no intent of acting on those thoughts, it could be counterproductive to immediately call the police. Consider other steps first, such as advising the person's therapist of the situation.

- Don't dare the person to kill herself. This is never helpful.

- Don't lecture or shame the person about having suicidal thoughts. Now is the time to listen, not to criticize, judge, or lecture her about why life is worthwhile. Your role is to be supportive and help connect the suicidal person with appropriate resources, not to be her therapist or to talk her out of it.

- Don't swear yourself to secrecy. If someone is actively at risk for suicide, you may need to involve someone else, and you can't afford to keep the person's condition secret. You don't want to be in a situation in which you keep the secret but lose the friend. What if you've already promised that you'd keep someone's suicidal thoughts a secret, and you're feeling stuck? This is an extremely difficult situation, but it's okay to go back to the person and say something like "I'm so sorry. I know that I promised you that I'd keep our conversation to myself, but I had no idea you were going to tell me you were thinking about dying. I'm really worried for you, and I need to get someone else involved because I'm not sure how to help make sure you're safe." Your friendship may temporarily suffer, but at least you're making it more likely that your friend will still be there in the future so you can work through this.

- In the unfortunate, rare event that someone threatens imminent suicide unless you do or don't do something for her, this is a dangerous situation that you shouldn't be expected to manage on your own. Don't let yourself be blackmailed or manipulated. Rather than getting drawn deeper into the situation, it's okay to say something like "I'm sorry, but I don't know how to be supportive when I feel that I'm being threatened. I need to consult with someone about what to do next." At that point, you should involve someone with more expertise—either by calling the person's therapist, doctor, or psychiatrist or by calling the police or 911.

SUMMARY

Suicidal thoughts are among the most serious symptoms of depression. Depressed people often view the world with such hopelessness and sadness that death may seem like their only relief from suffering. The important thing to remember is that most suicidal people do not want to die as much as they want relief, which means that there's realistic hope for treatment to work. Most suicide victims were dealing with depression or another mental illness at the time, and because these illnesses are treatable, suicide is mostly preventable. If you're caring for a friend or loved one who is suicidal, there are many ways to be supportive without feeling overly responsible for her life. What's important is to keep the lines of communication open and talk honestly about what she needs and how you can help. If you're the one having suicidal thoughts, it's important for you to stay in treatment and to find ways of letting the people in your life know how they can help you. In chapter 7, I'll focus on some additional ways of identifying what you need and how you can talk with others about how they can help.

CHAPTER 7

GETTING THE
SUPPORT YOU NEED

When you're recovering from depression, it's important that you be honest with yourself about needing extra support. In this chapter, I'll talk about identifying what you need and meeting those needs effectively. Like solving any difficult life situation, this requires you to do two different tasks at the same time: accept your current limitations, and do the best you can with the resources and energy that you have. In chapter 5, I mentioned the inner work of temporarily changing your expectations of yourself by accepting the reality of your symptoms; here, I'll talk about the outer work of taking action and getting social support for yourself.

THE IMPORTANCE OF TAKING ACTION TO GET SUPPORT FROM OTHERS

Why am I putting such a strong focus on getting what you need from other people? Because meeting our basic needs is central to having a healthy emotional life, and we need other people to help us meet those needs. As much as we like to feel independent, we're not islands. Each of us depends deeply on those around us to meet our basic needs. As infants, we're helpless and have to be fed, protected, and loved. Our need for connection and love is just as fundamental as our need for food, water, and shelter. When we can't rely on the world to meet these needs, our emotional lives can become depleted, flat, and empty. Growing up doesn't mean that we leave these needs behind, either. No matter how independent we like to think we are, we're deeply enmeshed in a world of intertwined social relationships. I've covered how to cope with some of these issues yourself in the discussion on symptom management in chapter 5. Here, I'll cover those needs that involve other people.

IDENTIFYING WHAT YOU NEED FROM OTHERS

Even though we all have common human needs for closeness and love, we meet these needs in different ways. An introverted, intellectual scientist is obviously not going to meet his needs for closeness in the same way that an outgoing entertainer would. We all have different styles. What I'd like to do first is give you a chance to reflect on what your specific needs are, then I'll talk about how you might go about meeting those needs. You might not know where to begin, so here are some questions you can ask yourself to help identify the kinds of things you might need.

Physical Proximity and Contact

- Do you want to spend more time with a particular friend, family member, or loved one? Conversely, are there any groups or responsibilities you temporarily need to disengage from while you're recovering?

- Are you part of any groups or organizations, such as religious groups, sports teams, or social clubs? What arrangements do you need to work out with them while you're recovering?

- What about your needs for affection and sex? If you have a lower sex drive while you're depressed, are there other ways to stay connected with your partner? Do you need to change your usual pattern of romantic or sexual activity for a while?

- If you're at risk for isolating yourself, do you want someone to call, stop by, or reach out to you? When and how often?

Talking and Communication

- Remember that it's your business whether you tell someone that you're depressed. Whom might you want to tell, and whom would you rather not tell? It's a balance between your privacy and the need to let people know that you're temporarily not at 100 percent. Remember that people aren't psychic and won't change their expectations of you unless you find a way to talk about what you need.

- You can't assume that other people will magically know how you're doing. Do you want your friends to check in with you to see how you're feeling from time to time, or would that only bother you?

Expectations for Work and Home

- How is your depression affecting your work? Are you having a harder time keeping up with certain responsibilities and expectations? List some of your specific problems.

- If you work in a job that offers sick leave or vacation time, is this an appropriate time to use that time away from work to recover? Do you need to ask for time off to make appointments with your therapist or doctor? Does your job offer flex time or other accommodations that might be useful?

- If you work in the home or can't take time away from your responsibilities at home, is it time to temporarily renegotiate what you're expected to do in terms of chores, cooking, cleaning, entertaining, child care, or other household responsibilities? Consider what you *are* able to do so that you can stay engaged and helpful.

- If you're a student, do you need to ask for some extensions on your work, or perhaps take a lighter load? Is there any benefit to taking a medical leave so you can focus on getting better?

Responding to Symptoms

- Do you need to go to bed at a different time than you used to?

- Are there particular foods that you just don't find appetizing anymore? Do you need to change what you're eating for a while? Do you need some assistance shopping for things that you need?

- If you're having problems with concentration, do you need reminders about certain activities or responsibilities?

- If you're feeling overwhelmed or indecisive, do you need some additional support with making plans?

- Do you need help in locating a therapist or psychiatrist? Do you need help finding transportation to your appointments?

ASKING FOR WHAT YOU NEED

After you've put some thought into what kinds of things you might need when you're recovering, it's time to think about how to ask for them. When you're asking others to help you out, they will of course be curious about why you're asking. Depending on what you ask for, some might even express concern. It's important, then, to think about how you want to explain your depression to other people, if at all.

When it comes to letting someone know you're depressed, remember that people can't read your mind. Giving others a framework for why you're making a particular request is a good way to help them understand where you're coming from, and they're more likely to help you out. You'll want to weigh the benefits against your privacy and the likely effect on your relationship.

For instance, one of the first choices you might need to make is whether you want to tell anyone in your family that you're dealing with depression. If you live with family, they can be in the best position to provide support and assistance. If they're close to you, they may have already noticed that you haven't been feeling like yourself, which may make it easier (and more important) to talk with them.

With people you're less close to, though, you may find it more important to err on the side of privacy. There might be situations in which it's not a good idea to let someone know that you're depressed. If someone is generally critical or judgmental or has made negative or blaming comments about people with emotional struggles, be careful with what you disclose. As important as it can be to be open about what you need, you do not want to open yourself to being shamed by someone who views depression as a weakness or a moral failing. Use your best judgment.

You don't even have to use the word "depression" if you don't want to. Let's consider some different ways of asking for the same thing—for instance, suppose you've been fatigued and need to go to bed earlier than usual. Also suppose that your family (or housemates) are used to you staying up and watching TV with them in the evenings. How might you explain this change in your behavior to them?

You could avoid mentioning anything out of the ordinary at all and just say, "Okay, I'm going to bed now." This approach certainty maximizes your privacy but would probably confuse or concern your family or housemates. Since you're not giving them any context for your behavior, they may make incorrect assumptions about why you're going to bed early. This kind of approach is unlikely to be helpful in the long run with people who are close to you. In relationships that aren't as important to you, though, this approach might work sometimes, because it just focuses on what you need without going into the details.

A more open approach might consist of saying "I've been tired lately and need to get some more sleep. Sorry, I'm just not up to watching TV with you guys tonight." This gives a little more information and shows some awareness of how your request is affecting other people. It's more self-disclosing and is likely to invite some natural care and concern from others.

An even more open approach might go like this: "Listen, I want you all to know that I've been having a hard time with feeling fatigued lately. I'm going to need to go to bed earlier for a while, and that means I probably won't be able to hang out with you as much. It's nothing personal; I just haven't had much energy for a while now, and I need to do this to take care of myself. When I'm feeling better, I'll look forward to hanging out like we usually do." This gives a much clearer context for what you're dealing with and helps set the stage for later conversations about what you need.

Finally, at the most self-disclosing end of the spectrum, you might want to disclose that your fatigue is part of a bigger picture. For instance, you might say, "I want you to know that I've been dealing with depression for a few weeks now. I'm getting the help I need, and part of that means getting some more rest and going to bed earlier than I used to. I'm doing my best to cope with the symptoms, but for now I just need you to understand why I'm not spending as much time with you." This approach gives the most information and context and would appropriately open the door to further conversations about what you need and how others can help. The more open you are, the more likely it is that others will be open and responsive in kind.

Remember, there's not a right answer here; the approach you take should be based on what you need and how your request will affect the people you talk with.

Special Case: Talking with Employers

If you work outside the home, it can be very challenging to know how to balance the demands of your job with the limitations that depression can cause. Remember that depression isn't just a disorder that affects your mood; it has very real cognitive effects that can make it difficult for you to think clearly, concentrate, or remember details. This can make work particularly challenging.

The question of whether or not to disclose your depression to your employer is complicated, because you may not know whether your employer will be supportive. There's no shame in dealing with depression, but the reality is that some people still attach a stigma to it. The less sure you are about your employer's attitudes, the more you should err on the side of caution by not immediately using the word "depression." You can always give more detail later if you need to, but until you're certain of being supported, stick with making limited and specific requests for what accommodations you need on the job. If pressed, you could also talk about being ill, without going into more detail.

Your employer is probably not allowed to ask you whether you're depressed but *can* ask you whether you're able to meet the requirements of your job. If your depressive symptoms are getting in the way of performing your job, you should consider talking with your human resources department about requesting reasonable accommodations. Courts have usually agreed that depression is a valid disability under the Americans with Disabilities Act (ADA); it is therefore usually a valid basis for requesting reasonable accommodations. If you're not sure which accommodations would be helpful, see the online resources in chapter 10 to get some ideas.

If you worry that your employer is unfairly discriminating against you just because you're depressed, you should consult with someone knowledgeable in employment law. Again, your workplace's human resources department can help you here. See chapter 10 for more information and resources to support you on this.

SUMMARY

Getting adequate social support begins within yourself when you accept how your symptoms are affecting you and that you could benefit from others' assistance. It's important that you think through how your symptoms have compromised your ability to live your life, do your work, fulfill your expectations for yourself, and meet your usual needs. Once you have an idea of how depression has affected you, think of what you need to get back on track and how the important people in your life can help. I provided some examples of how you might ask for their help while balancing the dual needs of protecting your privacy and communicating openly. A special case involves talking with your employer about particular accommodations you might need at work.

In the next chapter, I'll focus on another particular type of symptom management: managing other conditions that commonly occur together with depression.

CHAPTER 8

COMORBID CONDITIONS: DEPRESSION'S ROOMMATES

By now, you have some ideas about managing depressive symptoms—but there's more to know. Depression often doesn't occur in isolation; it's very common for people with depression to have other psychiatric problems as well. When someone is diagnosed with multiple psychiatric conditions at the same time, we call these comorbid conditions. I'll focus in this chapter on helping you identify and pursue proper treatment for some of the most common comorbid conditions.

SUBSTANCE ABUSE

It makes sense that depression and substance abuse often go hand in hand. It's easy to turn to alcohol or other drugs to cope with the feeling of hopelessness and guilt that depression can bring—and this can lead to a vicious circle. It could even be the case that using certain substances makes people more vulnerable to illnesses like depression. Regardless of causality, substance abuse and psychiatric diagnoses occur together so frequently that the term *dual diagnosis* was coined to refer to this phenomenon.

How do you know whether you're abusing a certain substance? Any time your substance use leads to personal, legal, social, or medical problems, you should be concerned. Defining a problem isn't about counting numbers of drinks, or the quantities of substances that you use, because different people have different tolerance levels. Instead, it's about honestly looking at how your substance use affects your life. If you find yourself needing to drink or use a drug to get through the day, or if you begin having cravings or withdrawal symptoms, you may have even crossed from abuse into dependence. Either one is serious, and you should always talk with a qualified physician or mental health provider about stopping. Substance abuse can cause difficulties on its own, but when you're dealing with depression at the same time, your ability to recover may be in jeopardy.

Combined Treatments for Substance Abuse and Depression

How might treatment for a substance problem combine with treatment for depression? At one extreme, if you have a serious substance problem, you might consider inpatient treatment focused primarily on treating your alcohol or drug use. This is sometimes called *detox* or *rehab* and usually takes place at a hospital or dedicated rehabilitation facility. If you pursue this route, you should be proactive in asking how treating your depression will be part of your overall treatment plan.

If your substance abuse is not severe, you might pursue outpatient substance abuse treatment and depression treatment concurrently. In some cases the same doctor or mental health provider might provide both treatments, but more likely you'd be seeing someone different for each type. For example, you might be in therapy for depression once a week and then attend individual or group therapy for substance abuse at a different time.

What kinds of treatments are available for substance abuse? There are different treatment philosophies, and they range from promoting complete abstinence (like Alcoholics Anonymous [AA], Narcotics Anonymous, and other 12-step programs) to advocating controlled drinking. Some programs use a regular group format, while others are less formal and more individualistic. I'll provide a broader list of recovery organizations, including alternatives to 12-step programs, in chapter 10. Regardless of the format, it's extremely important that you keep your primary mental health care provider informed of how your recovery is going.

You should also be sure to talk about how alcohol and other substances might interact with any medication you're taking.

ANXIETY DISORDERS

We all feel afraid, worried, or nervous sometimes, but if these experiences begin to interfere with our lives, they might be considered *anxiety disorders*. There are numerous kinds of anxiety disorders, but they share the common theme of preoccupation with managing experiences of worry, distress, or fear in ways that inadvertently prolong the fear or make it worse. Anxiety disorders are one of the most common comorbid conditions in people with depression (Hirschfeld 2001).

For instance, you've probably heard of *phobias*, which are irrational fears of certain things like animals or needles or certain situations like crowds or heights. It's common for someone who has never received professional help in this regard to manage a phobia by relying heavily on avoidance—that is, going to extremes to avoid the feared situation. The problem is that even though avoidance works great in making you feel safe and protected, it deprives you of an important opportunity to get over your fear. Worse, you come to believe that your avoidance was what protected you, so you're more likely to rely on it again when you feel anxious. As a result, avoidance in the short run intensifies anxiety in the long run. Avoidance, whether literal (leaving the room) or symbolic (obsessive hand washing to alleviate fears of contamination), is a key feature of anxiety disorders.

These disorders are some of the most common problems that can be comorbid with depression. By some estimates, up to 85 percent of people with depression also deal with significant anxiety symptoms (Gorman 1996/1997). This is an extremely high rate of co-occurrence and highlights the need for a comprehensive evaluation by a mental health professional to design an effective treatment plan. Let's look at some of the ways that anxiety and depression can reinforce each other and what combined treatment might look like.

Depression and Anxiety Can Worsen One Another

How can depression and anxiety interact with each other? I mentioned earlier that *avoidance* is the coping style that perpetuates anxiety; when avoidance is coupled with depression, the result is often interpersonal isolation. Isolation is just another form of avoidance and can easily start to reinforce itself. Just as someone who is afraid of dogs will come to believe that avoiding dogs is what keeps her safe, someone who is socially isolated may come to believe that being alone is the best way to cope with feelings of discomfort. In people diagnosed with both depression and anxiety, there is some evidence that symptoms of anxiety developed first (Kessler et al. 2003), so in these cases the tendency to cope via avoidance possibly is already learned by the time the person gets depressed.

The cognitive distortions that accompany anxiety and depression are also similar. For instance, it's easy to draw incorrect and unhealthy conclusions from depressive symptoms. A depressed person might begin to spend time alone and then mistakenly interpret her loneliness to mean that others don't want to be around her. As a result, the person is likely to feel worthless and continue to isolate herself.

What kinds of treatment are likely to help? You may recall from chapter 3 that cognitive therapy (CT) and cognitive behavioral therapy (CBT) are common types of psychotherapy used in treating depression. Fortunately, research suggests that CBT is also extremely effective in treating many anxiety disorders, so you can gain the skills to question and challenge the faulty perceptions and beliefs underlying both problems. Even better, CBT is highly structured and often relies on homework assignments to help keep avoidance from becoming a problem.

There is also initial evidence suggesting that interpersonal psychotherapy (IPT), a common and effective therapy for depression, may be useful in treating social phobia, a particular type of anxiety disorder marked by fear of many common social situations (Lipsitz et al. 1999). If your anxieties focus mostly on social situations, you might consider trying IPT as a way of treating your depression and getting valuable exposure to social situations. If your anxieties are not particularly related to social events, ask your therapist which would make more sense for you: IPT or a cognitive behavioral approach.

Several antidepressant medications also seem to have beneficial effects in treating anxiety. The classes of medications called selective serotonin reuptake inhibitors (SSRIs) and selective norepinephrine reuptake inhibitors (SNRIs) are very commonly prescribed for both depression and anxiety. If you're taking antidepressant medication, be sure to let your prescriber know if you also deal with symptoms of anxiety and how those symptoms are responding to your medication.

PERSONALITY DISORDERS

Having a "personality disorder" doesn't mean you're a horrible person. Mental health professionals use this term to describe the problems that result when a person's style of interacting with the world is too rigid. People with personality disorders often have a limited repertoire of ways of responding to life events and people in their lives, and they tend to have problems experiencing themselves and others as deeply and richly as they could.

Knowing about personality disorders is important because they're very common in people with depression (Gabbard and Simonsen 2007). One study by Shea and colleagues (1992) even suggested that among depressed people, between 23 and 87 percent also meet the criteria for at least one personality disorder, with higher numbers seen among inpatients diagnosed with depression. This is a staggeringly high degree of overlap and has important implications for treatment.

There are several kinds of personality disorders. For instance, someone with *narcissistic personality disorder* might see others primarily as people to impress, not as important people in their own right. As another example, people with *paranoid personality disorder* tend to be suspicious and see themselves as persecuted and attacked much of the time. We all like to impress others sometimes, and we can all feel suspicious sometimes, but when these tendencies are so strong that they dominate most of your relationships and interactions, they suggest a personality disorder.

One of the most common personality disorders—and one that frequently overlaps with depression—is *borderline personality disorder*. People with this disorder commonly have difficulty holding on to stable views of themselves and others, and they can rapidly shift between loving and hating feelings. They're often preoccupied with avoiding abandonment and can find themselves acting desperately and impulsively if they feel like their relationships are threatened. It's even common for people with this diagnosis to struggle with urges to harm, cut, or even kill themselves. The rapid emotional changes that accompany this disorder can make accurate diagnosis of depression difficult.

Not surprisingly, then, depressed people who are also diagnosed with a personality disorder will likely face more challenges in responding to treatment than people who have only depression. There are numerous possible explanations for this, ranging from interpersonal attachment problems in early life, to more severely distorted views of the world, to more difficulties in complying with treatment. In general, treating personality disorders takes longer than treating depression by itself and usually requires a more intensive kind of treatment. Treatment is still effective, but you should give yourself a much longer time frame for working through the problems caused by the personality disorder—often on the order of years rather than months.

What should you do if your mental health provider suggests that you're dealing with a personality disorder? This probably suggests that you've had some difficulties in your life because you find it hard to be flexible in certain situations. Depending on your specific diagnosis, you might find it useful to enter more intensive psychotherapy designed to help you learn some more flexible coping strategies and ways of looking at yourself and others. I would also suggest consulting with a psychiatrist or psychologist about the most appropriate course of therapy, instead of a primary care physician, because mental health specialists receive more training in diagnosing and treating personality disorders.

SUMMARY

Even though we can meaningfully talk about depression as an illness unto itself, in real life it's extremely common for people with depression to also have other medical and psychiatric diagnoses at the same time. This makes proper diagnosis and treatment planning particularly important, beginning with a medical checkup and then continuing with a thorough review for other possible psychiatric diagnoses. We've covered some of the most common psychiatric diagnoses here because they have important implications for treatment planning. Some problems, such as anxiety disorders, can be treated with psychotherapeutic techniques similar to those used to treat depression, while other problems, such as personality disorders and substance abuse, will likely require more specific and intensive treatment for symptom relief. Dealing with a comorbid diagnosis may make treatment take longer, but treatment can still be effective and is important to pursue. As Gabbard and Simonsen (2007, p. 172) state about comorbid conditions, "treatment is not futile, just lengthier."

CHAPTER 9

CARING FOR YOURSELF AFTER THE DEPRESSIVE EPISODE IS OVER

Remember that the term "depressive episode" means the period during which you have enough symptoms to interfere significantly with your life. I'll focus in this chapter on what happens when the dust settles and your depressive episode is over. Of course, it can feel great—but this is still a critical time that requires thoughtful attention. Give yourself two main goals during this time: preventing relapse, and readjusting to your life without depression.

RELAPSE AND RECURRENCE

Sadly, most people who have a depressive episode will have another one sometime in their lives. If you have another depressive episode within six months of the end of your previous episode, this is called a relapse. This basically means that the depressive episode didn't fully end. If you have a depressive episode more than six months after the previous episode, this is called a recurrence. This usually means that the previous depressive episode is considered to have ended, and you're now facing a new, separate episode. Recurrence rates for depression are very high: without treatment, between 25 and 40 percent of people will have a recurrence within two years. The incidence of recurrence rises to about 60 percent within five years, 75 percent within ten years, and close to 90 percent within fifteen years (Nierenberg, Petersen, and Alpert 2003; Keller and Boland 1998). The boundaries between relapse and recurrence aren't so black and white in real life. There's nothing magic about the six-month mark. Don't worry too much about the difference; just remember that depression tends to come back, and you need to be proactive about making sure that it doesn't. Even though relapse and recurrence can make depression especially demoralizing, the good news is that there are some important things you can do to help protect yourself against future episodes.

CONTINUATION TREATMENT AND MAINTENANCE TREATMENT

I'll start with the concept of *continuation treatment*. This just means continuing your treatment for depression (medication, therapy, or both) for at least several months after the depressive episode is over. Once you're no longer depressed, you shouldn't immediately stop your treatment; instead, you need to talk with your providers about what you should do to help prevent relapse. Your provider will likely recommend that you continue on medication or in therapy for a while after you're no longer depressed. You may wonder whether this is necessary, but there's evidence that continuation treatment can help reduce the likelihood of relapse and recurrence (Dunner et al. 2007). The window of six to nine months after a depressive episode is particularly critical, and to be on the safe side I often encourage depressed clients to consider the first year after an episode to be a time of heightened risk for relapse and recurrence.

Maintenance Psychotherapy

After a successful period of continuation therapy, there is value in receiving ongoing therapy—not for symptom relief, but to prevent another depressive episode (Dunner et al. 2007). Certain kinds of psychotherapy seem to be helpful in preventing relapse. Interpersonal psychotherapy (IPT) and cognitive behavioral therapy (CBT) have each shown moderate benefits in delaying relapse (Frank et al. 1991; Fava et al. 1998; Jarrett et al. 2001).

A newer therapy called mindfulness-based cognitive therapy (MBCT) also seems to reduce relapse in people who have had three or more depressive episodes (Teasdale et al. 2000). Regardless of the kind of therapy, the goal of maintenance psychotherapy is to help you continue coping with life stresses that may trigger another depressive episode.

Maintenance Medication

If you're taking antidepressant medication, your physician or psychiatrist will probably recommend that you continue to do so for a while even after you're no longer depressed. It's natural to want to stop taking a medication once you feel like you don't need it anymore, but you should always talk with your prescriber to find out how long you should continue taking it.

You shouldn't decide on your own to stop taking a medication; it's crucial to seek medical advice before stopping. Quitting certain antidepressant medications cold turkey can sometimes cause serious side effects, and you should always ask for medical advice when discontinuing a medication.

Will you need to stay on medication indefinitely? Probably not. Geddes and colleagues (2003) found that continuing medication after the end of a depressive episode significantly reduces relapse, and this finding appeared to hold for at least a year after the initial depressive episode was over. For those at higher risk of recurrence, though, they suggested that a year or more on maintenance medication may be beneficial. For some people, however, the risk of recurrence is so high that lifelong maintenance medication may be recommended. In particular, people who have had more than three depressive episodes or a protracted depressive episode (lasting more than two years) may need to consult with their doctors about the wisdom of staying on medication for life (Nierenberg, Petersen, and Alpert 2003). Lifelong medication might be a frustrating prospect, but remember that each subsequent depressive episode runs the risk of being longer, more severe, and more difficult to treat than the previous one.

Remember that if you treat your depression with medication alone, you may have residual symptoms once treatment is over. Conceptually, this makes sense, because even though antidepressant medications tend to work well, no medication can teach you the coping skills, resilience, and personal growth that can help forestall further depressive episodes. Another way of thinking about this is that once you stop taking a medication, it cannot provide any further protective benefits. The bottom line is just to keep an eye on yourself after discontinuing antidepressant medication, and be sure to talk with your prescriber to know when you may need to consider resuming treatment.

Knowing When to Seek Help Again

Once you've completed your treatment regimen and any recommended maintenance treatment, what's next? This is a good place to be, but you should think about the circumstances under which you should consider getting back into treatment. If you begin developing depressive symptoms again later in your life, don't wait until you meet the full criteria for a depressive episode!

By then it will be harder to treat, and you'll have missed out on the opportunity to prevent a full-blown episode. Instead, have a lower threshold for seeking help.

Think about how you first knew you were depressed—did you feel sad, empty, or anxious? Were there changes in your sleep or your appetite? Be on the lookout for those same changes. You don't need to be hypervigilant: remember that everyone has a miserable day or a sleepless night sometimes. But do pay attention to the number of symptoms, their severity and duration, and their effect on your life. If you start having several symptoms that last longer than you think they should, and if those symptoms start interfering with your life, go ahead and talk with your mental health professional again to see whether there's a need to resume treatment. It can be extremely helpful to maintain a chart of your energy, sleep, mood, and activities as discussed in chapter 5 so that you can spot downward trends before they get too severe.

Maintaining Social Support

In addition to managing symptoms, you can also help protect yourself against future depression by regularly participating in relationships. Satisfying, meaningful relationships are rewarding in their own right and are a great way to protect against the isolation that can lead to a recurrence of depression. This doesn't mean that you have to become a touchy-feely person if that's not your style. Even if you're introverted and don't like opening up to others, there are real benefits to just being around other people. Interestingly, even just being part of a sports team can help protect some people against depression (Babiss and Gangwisch 2009). Being part of a group, feeling valued for your contributions, and taking part in causes and activities larger than yourself are great ways to have more meaning and purpose in your life. Anything you can do to prevent isolation will likely help protect against relapse or recurrence.

What about online support groups? Connecting with other people recovering from depression can be a wonderful way of sharing information, getting support, and remembering that you're not alone. Even though connecting with others online can be helpful, the act of using a computer is generally a solitary activity, so you need to watch out for inadvertent isolation. It's also important not to spend too much time online. Submerging yourself in an online world at the expense of your real-world relationships is unlikely to meet your needs for real connection.

DAILY SELF-CARE

When you're recovering from depression, it's especially important for you to have some routine in your life. This doesn't mean having a boring, predictable lifestyle, but it does mean taking care of yourself by having a regular bedtime; consistent, healthy meals; and, ideally, a program of exercise.

Sleep

Getting regular, high-quality sleep is important on its own, and it can be even more important when you're recovering from depression. Among adolescents, getting more than eight hours of sleep per night was correlated with a significant reduction in the likelihood of becoming depressed; adolescents who got fewer than five hours of sleep per night were much more likely to deal with depression (Gangwisch et al. 2010). Even though the exact effects of sleep on relapse in depression have not been studied well, we do know that poor-quality sleep and insomnia are correlated with depression (Van Mill et al. 2010). Review the section in chapter 5 on coping with sleep problems for suggestions on keeping regular, healthy sleep habits.

Nutrition

Eating healthy food is important for its own reasons, and recall from chapter 5 that certain diets high in fruits, vegetables, and legumes and low in meats and dairy seem to provide some protection against depression. Recovery is an excellent time to begin committing to healthy eating habits, particularly ones that may protect against further depressive episodes.

Exercise

Beyond the well-known health benefits, research shows that moderate exercise can help reduce depressive symptoms and can even help reduce relapse. In 2000, Babyak and his colleagues found that people who did aerobic exercise for at least thirty minutes three times a week had a much lower rate of relapse than people who were on maintenance medication for depression.

Even better, these benefits lasted for months after the end of the initial depressive episode. The standard cautions apply about beginning any program of exercise—talk with your physician first if there are any complicating factors.

SUMMARY

Once you've had a depressive episode, you're likely to have another one sooner or later. Continuing with medication or therapy even after the depressive episode is over can help reduce the likelihood of recurrence, and there's even the option of ongoing maintenance treatment designed specifically to protect against recurrence. There are also many healthy lifestyle choices you can make to protect yourself even further. Keep a watchful eye on your symptoms, especially during the first year after the depressive episode, but you don't need to become fixated on monitoring yourself. Just have a low threshold for resuming treatment. Your recovery period may also be an excellent time to begin learning more about what you've been through and what you can do to prevent recurrence in the future. In the final chapter, I'll outline some resources for learning more about depression.

CHAPTER 10

ADDITIONAL
RESOURCES

When it comes to depression, good education and information about the illness are extremely important. In addition to the books and articles referenced in each chapter, I want to present some additional resources, mostly online resources, to help you get reliable, high-quality information about depression and its treatment.

HOW TO FIND RELIABLE HEALTH INFORMATION ONLINE

There's a lot of excellent information online about depression— and not surprisingly, there's a lot of misleading and inconsistent information as well (Eysenbach et al. 2002). How can you tell one from the other? Let's start off with a quick review of how to find good, high-quality information online.

When you're finding information online, always start by considering the source. Who is presenting the information, and does any individual or organization take responsibility for the accuracy of the information? If the information is anonymous or has no context, there's no way to verify how accurate it is. It's a step in the right direction if there's an identifiable person or organization taking responsibility for the health information, but this is still no guarantee of accuracy.

Next, ask why this person or organization is providing this information. Is it a government or nonprofit entity presenting information for the common good, or is it a commercial organization with a product or service to sell? You can get a clue by looking at the suffix of the domain in your browser's address bar: government agencies' websites usually end in ".gov", and noncommercial organizations' websites usually end in ".org". Commercial sites usually have the ".com" suffix. The most reliable health claims are given freely without being tied to any particular product or service. But remember—just because a claim is given freely doesn't mean that it's reliable!

Thinking Critically When Evaluating Online Health Information

Good critical thinking skills will take you far when evaluating health claims online. Astronomer Carl Sagan used to say, "Extraordinary claims require extraordinary evidence" (1980). If we apply this standard to getting health information online, then when someone makes a health claim that sounds too good to be true, you should expect them to provide lots of evidence to back up this claim. The best and most reliable evidence comes from scientific research published in peer-reviewed journals. That means that the person doing the research has opened up the work to scrutiny by other people in the field and that the work has been evaluated before publication.

Does the website seem to be sponsored by companies that might have an interest in the information being presented? For instance, if a website promotes a particular antidepressant, does the site have advertisements for that same drug? Even though bias is not always this obvious, this is a clue to a potential conflict of interest, and you should view that information more skeptically. All potential conflicts of interest should be clearly stated.

Does the website seem to make broad, sweeping claims without much evidence to back up what it says? Always look for where the information comes from—is it based in research, or is it someone's opinion? If the material is based on someone's opinion, how trustworthy is that opinion? It can be hard to tell, so look at the person's credentials. Does the person hold a professional license in the field? Has she done peer-reviewed research on the topic? What is her experience in this area?

How recent is the information? Certainly, some health information holds up over time, such as recommendations for good nutrition and sleep. If you're looking for information about medications, though, you'll likely want information that's as current as possible.

Some sources, such as healthfinder.gov, act as clearinghouses for reliable, pre-screened health information. Generally speaking, government health agencies and national professional organizations are likely to give reliable information. I'll list some below, but don't take anything these sites say (or that I say) for granted. Your own common sense and critical thinking skills are always your best guides.

National Organizations

The National Institute of Mental Health (nimh.nih.gov) is dedicated to finding effective treatments for psychiatric illnesses and can provide excellent information about most such illnesses.

The Substance Abuse and Mental Health Services Administration website (www.samhsa.gov) holds a wealth of information about treating numerous psychiatric diagnoses, particularly depression and substance abuse.

The American Psychological Association (apa.org) is the largest organization representing psychologists in the United States. The website offers many resources about the field of psychology for professionals and the public.

Similarly, the American Psychiatric Association (psych.org) is the largest professional psychiatric association in the world, and the website provides a wealth of information about psychiatry, usually from a medical perspective.

The National Alliance on Mental Illness (nami.org) is a nationwide organization that has worked since 1979 to improve the lives of people with psychiatric diagnoses.

For military veterans, the US Department of Veterans Affairs (www.vetcenter.va.gov) can offer help with the specific mental health needs of former service members.

CHAPTER 1: WHAT IS DEPRESSION?

Depression

The National Institute of Mental Health (NIMH) has clear, reliable information about depression online at nimh.nih.gov/health/publications/depression-easy-to-read/index.shtml.

The National Library of Medicine and the National Institutes of Health also provide clear, interactive presentations about depression at www.nlm.nih.gov/medlineplus/depression.html.

The *Journal of the American Medical Association* (JAMA) provides a document summarizing current information about depression at jama.ama-assn.org/content/303/19/1994.full.pdf.

It can be also very helpful to read about depression from a personal point of view to remind you that you're not alone. I recommend William Styron's *Darkness Visible* (1992), a touching account of the author's struggles with severe depression. Author Nell Casey has collected a book of twenty-two short, vibrant accounts of people living with depression called *Unholy Ghost* (1992). Two chapters are also written from the point of view of loved ones watching a family member deal with the illness, providing a touching account of how depression affects families and relationships. Finally, *The Noonday Demon* by Andrew Solomon (2002) is an insightful exploration of depression on personal and societal levels.

Bipolar Disorder

An outstanding self-help book for young adults diagnosed with bipolar disorder is Russ Federman and Andy Thomson's *Facing Bipolar: The Young Adult's Guide to Dealing with Bipolar Disorder* (2010). It's extremely practical and contains excellent advice for coping with this disorder.

One of the best personal accounts of living with bipolar disorder is psychiatrist Kay Redfield Jamison's *An Unquiet Mind* (1997). Rather than talk about the disorder from a detached, clinical perspective, she boldly talks about her own life and struggles with bipolar illness.

Specific Populations

For college students, Half of Us (www.halfofus.com) is an organization dedicated to combating depression and suicidal thinking. The website offers self-assessment instruments and excellent information on how to help a friend struggling with depression or suicidality.

For older adults, the Geriatric Mental Health Foundation (gmhfonline.org) offers excellent information about common mental health conditions.

CHAPTER 2: GETTING A CORRECT DIAGNOSIS

Finding a Therapist

In most cases, I recommend inquiring with your insurance company first to find local mental health providers who are covered under your plan. Call your insurer or see whether its website can provide access to a listing of covered local providers. Once you get a list, you can narrow it down by cross-referencing it with information you find about these providers online.

The American Psychological Association offers a therapist locator at locator.apa.org.

The American Association for Marriage and Family Therapy (www.aamft.org) also has a therapist locator service.

The Substance Abuse and Mental Health Services Administration (SAMHSA) provides an online service to locate local inpatient and outpatient mental health services at store.samhsa.gov/mhlocator.

The US Department of Veterans Affairs offers its own specialized service for veterans who are seeking local mental health services at va.gov/landing2_locations.htm.

For younger people, the American Academy of Child and Adolescent Psychiatry website (aacap.org) has a wealth of information for families. It also offers a service for locating specialists in child and adolescent psychiatry.

If you would prefer to speak with a pastoral counselor, who is trained in discussing spiritual issues in therapy, you can use the American Association of Pastoral Counselors website (aapc.org) to locate members of this organization.

Most credentialed mental health providers, such as licensed clinical social workers and professional counselors, are licensed by the states in which they practice. You can search online for your state's licensing board to find out whether a therapist is properly licensed. Remember that the generic terms "therapist" and "psychotherapist" are not regulated in most states and that anyone can use these titles, regardless of training.

CHAPTER 3: TREATMENTS FOR DEPRESSION

Mindfulness-Based Approaches to Treatment

Mindfulness-based cognitive therapy (mbct.com) is a structured group therapy for people who have had more than three depressive episodes and is designed to help prevent relapse.

If you prefer to do some reading on your own, a popular self-help book with a good research focus is Mark Williams, John Teasdale, Zindel Segal, and Jon Kabat-Zinn's *The Mindful Way through Depression: Freeing Yourself from Chronic Unhappiness* (2007). It contains a concise, jargon-free explanation of mindfulness and its application to coping with depression.

One of the most popular mindfulness-based programs designed for people coping with chronic stress or chronic illness, including depression, is mindfulness-based stress reduction (MBSR). MBSR began at the University of Massachusetts Medical School; you can learn more at umassmed.edu/cfm.

Interpersonal Psychotherapy for Depression

Although many therapists practice IPT, it is difficult to find a comprehensive listing. I would recommend contacting your insurance company or potential providers directly to ask whether they practice IPT.

The International Society for Interpersonal Psychotherapy (interpersonalpsychotherapy.org) is dedicated to training and education about IPT. The website contains excellent information about IPT but does not offer a therapist locator.

University of Iowa Hospitals and Clinics is home to the Interpersonal Psychotherapy Institute, which makes available excellent information about IPT for both patients and therapists. See iptinstitute.com. The institute also provides a limited directory of IPT practitioners in the United States and abroad at uihealthcare.com/depts/interpersonalpsycho therapyinstitute/mapoffaculty.html.

Cognitive Therapy and Cognitive Behavioral Therapy

The Academy of Cognitive Therapy (ACT) website (academyofct .org) contains a listing of ACT-certified therapists.

The Association for Behavioral and Cognitive Therapies (ABCT) website (abct.org) contains excellent information about CBT in general, and it provides a searchable listing of cognitive behavioral therapists.

An excellent supplement to CBT is David Burns's book *Feeling Good: The New Mood Therapy* (1999). I frequently recommend this classic in the field of CBT. It outlines the principles of cognitive behavioral treatment for depression in a clear and practical way, and it's full of practice exercises that you can use to hone your coping skills.

CHAPTER 4: MONITORING YOUR PROGRESS IN TREATMENT

You should keep track of your mood and depressive symptoms regularly; I advise checking in with yourself at least once a week using a standardized depression assessment instrument like the PHQ-9. You can take it online anonymously and for free at depression-screening.org.

The Mayo Clinic maintains a web page with excellent information about treatment-resistant depression at www.mayoclinic.com/health/treatment-resistant-depression/DN00016.

CHAPTER 5: MANAGING YOUR SYMPTOMS

Sleep

The National Sleep Foundation (www.sleepfoundation.org) provides information about getting better sleep, as well as information about many common sleep problems.

Nutrition

If you'd like to begin making healthy changes in the way you eat but aren't sure where to begin, start with the US Department of Agriculture's online service, www.choosemyplate.gov.

Mental Health America has an excellent web page on eating healthily while you're dealing with depression: liveyour-lifewell.org/go/live-your-life-well/eat.

CHAPTER 6: MANAGING SUICIDAL THOUGHTS

Helplines

If you have already taken action to end your life, such as taking an overdose of pills, then call 911 immediately.

If you are feeling suicidal, call the National Suicide Prevention Lifeline, a 24-hour toll-free number, at 1-800-273-TALK (8255). For non-emergency information, and information on helping a friend or loved one who may be suicidal, go to sui-cidepreventionlifeline.org.

The Trevor Project (www.thetrevorproject.org) is a suicide hot-line specializing in talking with gay, lesbian, bisexual, trans-gender, or questioning youth. The number is 1-866-4-U-TREVOR (1-866-488-7386).

Resources and Organizations

The American Academy of Suicidology (suicidology.org) offers information and training for people and agencies who want to help prevent suicide. It does not operate a helpline, but it does offer information to people who have had suicidal thoughts. It can also provide information about local crisis centers.

The Suicide Prevention Resource Center (sprc.org) has a wealth of information for those interested in learning more about dealing with life-threatening behavior.

The Jed Foundation (jedfoundation.org) is an outstanding suicide prevention resource for college students, parents of college students, and college personnel.

The National Organization for People of Color against Suicide (nopcas.org) provides resources especially for members of racial or ethnic minorities.

CHAPTER 7: GETTING THE SUPPORT YOU NEED

Employment Law and Discrimination

If you believe you've been discriminated against because you have depression or another psychiatric diagnosis, you can contact the federal Equal Opportunity Employment Commission (eeoc.gov) through the website or by calling 1-800-669-4000. The EEOC also has some current information about how the ADA is enforced when it comes to people with psychiatric diagnoses, at eeoc.gov/policy/docs/psych.html.

The Center for Psychiatric Rehabilitation at Boston University maintains several online resources for employers and employees who want to know more about ADA-compliant reasonable accommodations for psychiatric diagnoses. Start at www .bu.edu/cpr/reasaccom.

For how to file a discrimination complaint with the US Department of Education's Office for Civil Rights, see ed.gov /about/offices/list/ocr/docs/howto.html.

An excellent organization dedicated to promoting the legal and civil rights of people with psychiatric diagnoses is the Judge David L. Bazelon Center for Mental Health Law (bazelon .org). It maintains a listing of online resources at bazelon.org /News-Publications/Other-Resources/Other-Resources-about -Civil-Rights-and-the-ADA.aspx.

The Society for Human Resource Management (www.shrm.org) maintains an online database of articles and information for employers seeking to provide reasonable accommodations to employees with a disability.

Finding In-Person or Online Support

The Depression and Bipolar Support Alliance (www.dbsalliance
.org) is a national organization providing educational and
support materials to people diagnosed with mood disorders. It
also provides information about local support groups led by
people who have dealt with these diagnoses. The DBSA runs
a website designed to help you make a wellness plan while
you're recovering: www.facingus.org.

Getting Your Family Involved

Families for Depression Awareness (familyaware.org) is a national
organization with the mission of helping families learn effective ways of coping with depression and suicidality.

For Military Personnel

The Substance Abuse and Mental Health Services Administration
(SAMHSA) offers special information for service members
and their families at www.samhsa.gov/MilitaryFamilies.

CHAPTER 8: COMORBID CONDITIONS

Resources for Recovering from Alcohol Abuse

Alcoholics Anonymous (AA) is probably the best-known 12-step program, AA (aa.org) promotes abstinence through a one-day-at-a-time focus. It encourages regular, free group meetings and adherence to a 12-step plan. Though it denies any particular religious focus, be aware that AA often uses spiritual language, such as referring to a "higher power."

Moderation Management (MM) (moderation.org) differs from AA in several aspects of its treatment approach. It strives to reach people in the early stages of problem drinking, before full-blown alcohol abuse takes hold. Abstinence is not necessarily the goal for everyone in this model; members may choose to reduce their drinking instead.

Rational Recovery (RR), unlike the group settings promoted through AA or MM, emphasizes individual efforts to recover from alcohol abuse. It provides support through its website (rational.org) and teaches techniques for identifying unhealthy patterns and cravings.

SMART (Self Management and Recovery Training) Recovery (smartrecovery.org) offers online and face-to-face groups and encourages abstinence but does not follow a 12-step model. It emphasizes problem-solving and coping with urges.

Other Drugs of Abuse

The National Institute on Drug Abuse (drugabuse.gov) is a federal agency providing reliable, current information about treating substance abuse disorders.

There are also many organizations that use the "anonymous" model of group support, meaning that you do not have to give your full name in order to participate in the groups. Some of the more popular organizations are:

- Cocaine Anonymous (ca.org)

- Marijuana Anonymous (marijuana-anonymous.org)

- Crystal Meth Anonymous (www.crystalmeth.org)

Anxiety Disorders

The Anxiety Disorders Association of America website (adaa .org) is an excellent source of information about anxiety disorders and their treatment.

Personality Disorders

In recent years, a specific type of therapy called dialectical behavioral therapy (DBT) has emerged as a proven way to treat many of the problems that accompany personality disorders, particularly borderline personality disorders. Developed by psychologist Marsha Linehan, DBT focuses on teaching practical skills in regulating difficult emotions, learning effective interpersonal skills, and managing emotional distress. I often use Matthew McKay, Jeffrey Wood, and Jeffrey Brantley's *Dialectical Behavior Therapy Skills Workbook* (2007) to introduce these concepts—it's full of practical exercises to build resilience.

Other types of therapy that have been shown to be effective in treating personality disorders are transference-focused psychotherapy (TFP), a psychodynamic treatment focused on changing maladaptive views of the self and others, and mentalization-based treatment, which focuses on differentiating between one's own thoughts and feelings and the thoughts and feelings of others. You can locate more information about these types of therapy online, but note that many of the sites are geared toward professionals.

CHAPTER 9: CARING FOR YOURSELF AFTER THE DEPRESSIVE EPISODE IS OVER

Mental Health America provides an online version of the PHQ-9, the depression screening tool used earlier in this book, at depression-screening.org. It can help you monitor your emotional health from time to time while you're in recovery.

Another site created by this same organization, liveyourlifewell .org/go/live-your-life-well/ways, contains ten tools you can use to care for yourself and maintain healthy relationships.

SUMMARY

I hope these resources deepen your understanding of what depression is and how you can protect yourself against future episodes. Recovering from depression takes time, patience, and determination, and I hope you can be proud of the efforts you've made to help yourself. Ideally, you've come to understand yourself better and have some better ideas about how to take care of yourself when you struggle with depressive symptoms. More than anything else, I hope that you've been able to develop a deeper sense of compassion for yourself while you are recovering and that you can extend that compassion to other people in your life who may be fighting their own battles.

REFERENCES

Babiss, L. A., and J. E. Gangwisch. 2009. Sports participation as a protective factor against depression and suicidal ideation in adolescents as mediated by self-esteem and social support. *Journal of Developmental and Behavioral Pediatrics* 30 (5): 376–84.

Babyak, M. A., J. A. Blumenthal, S. Herman, P. Khatri, P. M. Doraiswamy, K. A. Moore, W. E. Craighead, T. T. Baldewicz, and K. R. Krishnan. 2000. Exercise treatment for major depression: Maintenance of therapeutic benefit at 10 months. *Psychosomatic Medicine* 62 (5): 633–38.

Beck, A. T. 1986. Hopelessness as a predictor of eventual suicide. *Annals of New York Academy of Sciences* 487: 90–96.

Boland, R. J., and M. B. Keller. 2002. Course and outcome of depression. In *Handbook of Depression*, edited by I. H. Gotlib and C. L. Hammen. New York: The Guilford Press.

Burns, D. D. 1999. *Feeling Good: The New Mood Therapy*. Revised and updated. New York: HarperCollins.

Casey, N., ed. 2002. *Unholy Ghost: Writers on Depression*. New York: Harper Perennial.

Dunner, D. L., P. Blier, M. B. Keller, M. H. Pollack, M. E. Thase, and J. M. Zajecka. 2007. Preventing recurrent depression: Long-term treatment for major depressive disorder. *Primary Care Companion to the Journal of Clinical Psychiatry* 9 (3): 214–23.

Eaddy, M., and T. Regan. 2003. Real world 6-month immediate-release SSRIs non-adherence. Paper presented at the Program and abstracts of the Disease Management Association of America 5th Annual Disease Management Leadership Forum, Chicago, IL.

Eysenbach, G., J. Powell, O. Kuss, and E.-R. Sa. 2002. Empirical studies assessing the quality of health information for consumers on the World Wide Web. *Journal of the American Medical Association* 287 (20): 2691–700.

Fava, G. A., C. Rafanelli, S. Grandi, S. Conti, and P. Belluardo. 1998. Prevention of recurrent depression with cognitive behavioral therapy: Preliminary findings. *Archives of General Psychiatry* 55 (9): 816–20.

Federman, R., and J. A. Thomson Jr. 2010. *Facing Bipolar: The Young Adult's Guide to Dealing with Bipolar Disorder*. Oakland, CA: New Harbinger Publications.

Frank, E., D. J. Kupfer, E. F. Wagner, A. B. McEachran, and C. Cornes. 1991. Efficacy of interpersonal psychotherapy as a maintenance treatment of recurrent depression. *Archives of General Psychiatry* 48 (12): 1053–59.

Freud, S. 1917. Mourning and melancholia. In *The Standard Edition of the Complete Psychological Works of Sigmund Freud, Volume XIV (1914–1916): On the History of the Psycho-Analytic Movement, Papers on Metapsychology and Other Works*, edited by J. Strachey. London: Hogarth Press.

Gabbard, G. O., and E. Simonsen. 2007. The impact of personality and personality disorders on the treatment of depression. *Personality and Mental Health* 1 (2): 161–75.

Gangwisch, J. E., L. A. Babiss, D. Malaspina, J. B. Turner, G. K. Zammit, and K. Posner. 2010. Earlier parental set bedtimes as a protective factor against depression and suicidal ideation. *Sleep* 33 (1): 97–106.

Geddes, J. R., S. M. Carney, C. Davies, T. A. Furukawa, D. J. Kupfer, E. Frank, and G. M. Goodwin. 2003. Relapse prevention with antidepressant drug treatment in depressive disorders: A systematic review. *Lancet* 361 (9358): 653–61.

González, H. M., W. A. Vega, D. R. Williams, W. Tarraf, B. T. West, and H. W. Neighbors. 2010. Depression care in the United States: Too little for too few. *Archives of General Psychiatry* 67 (1): 37–46.

Gorman, J. M. 1996/1997. Cormorbid depression and anxiety spectrum disorders. *Depression and Anxiety* 4 (4): 160–68.

Hayes, S. C., K. D. Strosahl, and K. G. Wilson. 2003. *Acceptance and Commitment Therapy: An Experiential Approach to Behavior Change*. New York: The Guilford Press.

Hirschfeld, R. M. A. 2001. The comorbidity of major depression and anxiety disorders: Recognition and management in primary care. *The Primary Care Companion to the Journal of Clinical Psychiatry* 3 (6): 244–54.

Hirshkowitz, M., C. A. Moore, and G. Minhoto. 1997. The basics of sleep. In *Understanding Sleep: The Evaluation and Treatment of Sleep Disorders*, edited by M. R. Pressman and W. C. Orr. Washington, DC: American Psychological Association.

Jamison, K. R. 1997. *An Unquiet Mind: A Memoir of Moods and Madness*. New York: Vintage.

Jarrett, R. B., D. Kraft, J. Doyle, B. M. Foster, G. G. Eaves, and P. C. Silver. 2001. Preventing recurrent depression using cognitive therapy with and without a continuation phase: A randomized clinical trial. *Archives of General Psychiatry* 58 (4): 381–88.

Jobes, D. A. 2006. *Managing Suicidal Risk: A Collaborative Approach*. New York: The Guilford Press.

Joiner, T. E. Jr. 2002. Depression in its interpersonal context. In *Handbook of Depression*, edited by I. H. Gotlib and C. L. Hammen. New York: The Guilford Press.

Keller, M. B., and R. J. Boland. 1998. Implications of failing to achieve successful long-term maintenance treatment of recurrent unipolar major depression. *Biological Psychiatry* 44 (5): 348–60.

Kessler, R. C., P. Berglund, O. Demler, R. Jin, D. Koretz, K. R. Merikangas, A. J. Rush, E. E. Walters, and P. S. Wang. 2003. The epidemiology of major depressive disorder: Results from the National Comorbidity Survey Replication (NCS-R). *Journal of the American Medical Association* 289 (23): 3095–105.

Kwahaja, I. S., J. J. Westermeyer, P. Gajwani, and R. E. Feinstein. 2009. Depression and coronary artery disease: The association, mechanisms, and therapeutic implications. *Psychiatry* (Edgemont) 6 (1): 38–51.

Linehan, M. 1993. *Cognitive-Behavioral Treatment of Borderline Personality Disorder.* New York: The Guilford Press.

Lipsitz, J. D., J. C. Markowitz, S. Cherry, and A. J. Fyer. 1999. Open trial of interpersonal psychotherapy for the treatment of social phobia. *American Journal of Psychiatry* 156 (11): 1814–16.

Ma, S. H., and J. D. Teasdale. 2004. Mindfulness-based cognitive therapy for depression: Replication and exploration of differential relapse prevention effects. *Journal of Consulting and Clinical Psychology* 72 (1): 31–40.

McKay, M., J. C. Wood, and J. Brantley. 2007. *Dialectical Behavior Therapy Skills Workbook: Practical DBT Exercises for Learning Mindfulness, Interpersonal Effectiveness, Emotion Regulation, and Distress Tolerance.* Oakland, CA: New Harbinger Publications.

Mitchell, A. J., A. Vaze, and S. Rao. 2009. Clinical diagnosis of depression in primary care: A meta-analysis. *Lancet* 374: 609–19.

Moore, T. H. M., S. Zammit, A. Lingford-Hughes, T. R. E. Barnes, P. B. Jones, M. Burke, and G. Lewis. 2007. Cannabis use and risk of psychotic or affective mental health outcomes: A systematic review. *Lancet* 370 (9584): 319–28.

Moussavi, S., S. Chatterji, E. Verdes, A. Tandon, V. Patel, and B. Ustun. 2007. Depression, chronic diseases, and decrements in health: Results from the World Health Surveys. *Lancet* 370 (9590): 851–58.

Mufson, L., K. P. Dorta, D. Moreau, and M. M. Weissman. 2004. *Interpersonal Psychotherapy for Depressed Adolescents*, 2nd ed. New York: Guilford Press.

Musty, R. E., and L. Kaback. 1995. Relationships between motivation and depression in chronic marijuana users. *Life Sciences* 56 (23–24): 2151–58.

Nierenberg, A. A., T. J. Petersen, and J. E. Alpert. 2003. Prevention of relapse and recurrence in depression: The role of long-term pharmacotherapy and psychotherapy. *Journal of Clinical Psychiatry* 64 (suppl. 15): 13–17.

Pan, A., M. Lucas, Q. Sun, R. M. van Dam, O. H. Franco, J. E. Manson, W. C. Willett, A. Ascherio, and F. B. Hu. 2010. Bidirectional association between depression and type 2 diabetes mellitus in women. *Archives of Internal Medicine* 170 (21): 1884–91.

Rogers, D., and R. Pies. 2008. General medical drugs associated with depression. *Psychiatry* (Edgemont) 5 (12): 28–41.

Ruhé, H. G., J. Huyser, J. A. Swinkels, and A. H. Schene. 2006. Switching antidepressants after a first selective serotonin reuptake inhibitor in major depressive disorder: A systematic review. *Journal of Clinical Psychiatry* 67 (12): 1836–55.

Rupke, S. J., D. Blecke, and M. Renfrow. 2006. Cognitive therapy for depression. *American Family Physician* 73 (1): 83–86.

Sagan, C. 1980. Encyclopaedia Galactica (episode aired December 14). *Cosmos*, PBS.

Sánchez-Villegas, A., M. Delgado-Rodriguez, A. Alonso, J. Schlatter, F. Lahortiga, L. S. Majem, and M. A. Martinez-González. 2009. Association of the Mediterranean dietary pattern with the incidence of depression. *Archives of General Psychiatry* 66 (10): 1090–98.

Shea, M. T., T. A. Widiger, and M. H. Klein. 1992. Comorbidity of personality disorders and depression: Implications for treatment. *Journal of Consulting and Clinical Psychology* 60 (6): 857–68.

Shedler, J. 2010. The efficacy of psychodynamic psychotherapy. *American Psychologist* 65 (2): 98–109.

Solomon, A. 2002. *The Noonday Demon: An Atlas of Depression.* New York: Scribner.

Spitzer, R. L., J. B. W. Williams, and K. Kroenke. 2001. The PHQ-9: Validity of a brief depression severity measure. *Journal of General Internal Medicine* 16 (9): 606–13.

Styron, W. 1992. *Darkness Visible: A Memoir of Madness.* New York: Vintage.

Teasdale, J. D., Z. V. Segal, J. M. G. Williams, V. Ridgeway, J. Soulsby, and M. Lau. 2000. Prevention of relapse/recurrence in major depression by mindfulness-based cognitive therapy. *Journal of Consulting and Clinical Psychology* 68 (4): 615–23.

Van Mill, J. G., W. J. Hoogendijk, N. Vogelzangs, R. van Dyck, and B. W. Penninx. 2010. Insomnia and sleep duration in a large cohort of patients with major depressive disorder and anxiety disorders. *Journal of Clinical Psychiatry* 71 (3): 239–46.

Wallace, J., T. Schneider, and P. McGuffin. 2002. Genetics of depression. In *Handbook of Depression*, edited by I. H. Gotlib and C. L. Hammen. New York: The Guilford Press.

Weissman, M. M., J. C. Markowitz, and G. L. Klerman. 2000. *Comprehensive Guide to Interpersonal Psychotherapy*. New York: Basic Books.

Weissman, M. M., J. C. Markowitz, and G. L. Klerman. 2007. *Clinicians Quick Guide to Interpersonal Psychotherapy*. Oxford: Oxford University Press.

White, J. L., and M. M. Mitler. 1997. The diagnostic interview and differential diagnosis for complaints of excessive daytime sleepiness. In *Understanding Sleep: The Evaluation and Treatment of Sleep Disorders*, edited by M. Hirshkowitz, C. A. Moore, and G. Minhoto. Washington, DC: American Psychological Association.

Williams, M., J. D. Teasdale, Z. V. Segal, and J. Kabat-Zinn. 2007. *The Mindful Way through Depression: Freeing Yourself from Chronic Unhappiness*. New York: The Guilford Press.

Lee H. Coleman, PhD, ABPP, is a clinical psychologist specializing in clinical work, outreach, supervision, and consultation to university populations. He is currently assistant director and director of training at the California Institute of Technology's student counseling center.

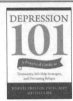